CAREER
AND
CALLING

CAREER
AND
CALLING

A Guide for Counselors, Youth, and Young Adults

Ginny Ward Holderness
with Forrest C. Palmer Jr.

Geneva Press
Louisville, Kentucky

Scripture quotations, unless otherwise indicated, are from the New Revised Standard Version of the Bible, copyright © 1989 by the Division of Christian Education of the National Council of the Churches of Christ in the U.S.A., and are used by permission. Scripture quotations marked (NIV) are from the Holy Bible, New International Version. Copyright © 1973, 1978, 1984 International Bible Society. Used by permission of Zondervan Bible Publishers.

Book design by Sharon Adams
Cover design by Pam Poll Graphic Design

First edition
Published by Geneva Press
Louisville, Kentucky

This book is printed on acid-free paper that meets the American National Standards Institute Z39.48 standard.♾

PRINTED IN THE UNITED STATES OF AMERICA

01 02 03 04 05 06 07 08 09 10 — 10 9 8 7 6 5 4 3 2 1

Library of Congress Cataloging-in-Publication Data

Holderness, Ginny Ward, 1946–
    Career and calling : a guide for counselors, youth, and young adults / Ginny Ward Holderness with Forrest
C. Palmer, Jr.— 1st ed.
        p. cm.
Includes bibliographical references
ISBN 0-664-50205-9 (alk. paper)
    1. Vocation—Christianity. 2. Pastoral counseling. 3. Vocational guidance. I. Palmer, Forrest C. (Forrest
Charles), 1950– II. Title.

BV4740 .H563 2000
253.5—dc21   00-060027

CONTENTS

100585

ACKNOWLEDGMENTS

Acknowledgments are not the most interesting part of a book for the readers, but they are a lot of fun for the authors. Though they are found at the front of a book, writing acknowledgments signals the end of hours of research, writing, and field testing. And they provide an opportunity to think about all the people for whom we are grateful. We can't name everyone, for there are teachers, mentors, young people, and young adults who are a part of this writing simply by being a part of our lives, our vocations, our callings.

This book began taking shape seven years before I ever thought it would be a book. Nine years ago I began taking young people from First Presbyterian Church, Dalton, to the Career Development Center of the Southeast in Decatur, Georgia, for two-day testing and counseling. The church got a break in cost if we did a precounseling program prior to our visit. We were sent materials published in 1974, which included an excellent student book by David P. Campbell, *If You Don't Know Where You're Going, You'll Probably End Up Somewhere Else.* Marilyn Allred, a counselor at the center, asked me if I'd be interested in updating the sessions. What began as a simple updating mushroomed, resulting in this book.

Forrest, who serves on the board of directors of the Career Development Center with me, joined the project, offering his Internet savvy and his willingness to research career counseling for those who have special needs. Forrest brought a sensitivity which recognizes that all God's children can be called by God.

I am grateful for the commitment of Marcy Szoboda and Rob Lively, lay leaders of Dalton First Presbyterian's counseling groups, who helped shape the career counseling sessions; and for the contributions of Earl Stewart and Alicia Phillips, counselors at the Career Development Center of the Southeast, and of our good friend Rodger Nishioka.

There are too many people to name whose stories have found their way into these pages. Forrest and I are grateful to all of you for sharing your experiences and your wisdom. Special thanks to my sisters-in-law and their husbands, Zelle and John Jester and Nancy and Tom Reams, who made their beach house available at exactly the right times when I needed to get a lot of writing done.

Forrest acknowledges with love his wife, Barb, and two sons, David and Tim, "who continue to experience God's call for us as a family." He is also grateful for "those who live with disabilities and inspire us through their abilities."

Finally, my deep appreciation goes to my husband, Jim, my resident theologian and constant support, and to our children, J.B. and Lorinda, who are in the process of living God's call.

ACKNOWLEDGMENT

Introduction

Young people today are having trouble answering the question they've been asked since they were five years old: "What do you want to do when you grow up?" They don't know. The future is overwhelming to a generation of youth who have more experiences, more interests, more abilities, and more available to them than any other generation. The problem intensifies with age, as many young adults, who are supposed to be settling into a career, are asking, "What do I want to do with my life?"

The problem with these questions is that they cover too much territory. A better question would be: "What do you want to do first?" This question removes the pressure of having to make one choice for a lifetime. It makes the task of career search manageable. It helps lessen the fear of making a mistake.

"What do you want to do first? or next?" is more in tune with the way things are. Statistics show that people change jobs an average of fourteen times. They change careers, that is, they move to totally different professions or fields, five to seven times. So it doesn't make sense to ask people to pick one career, when in all likelihood they will leave it and move on to something else.

The subject of this book is the unknown, the future, and how to get to it in a constructive way. What we have observed in interviews with both young people and young adults are two anticipations of the future. The first, which we expected, is that youth and young adults are anxious about their futures. The second reaction surprised and pleased us. Many members of this younger generation, in spite of not knowing what the future holds, are excited about it. They have a confidence and peace that God is in control and will guide them as they go. They face life with a joyful expectancy.

The purpose of career counseling ministry is to move people from fear and anxiety to this joyful expectancy about their futures. The church asks the vocational question a bit differently: "What is God calling you to be and to do both now and in the future?" "What is God calling you to be and do first? or next?" This question encourages people to think not just about what they do, their occupation, but about who they are. The church can offer young people and young adults an opportunity to discover who they are as God's beloved created ones, to recognize how God is present in their lives, and to explore the unique gifts, abilities, and interests that God has given them.

In both the secular and the sacred arena, good career counseling is less about helping people find a career and more about helping people know themselves. The better you know yourself, the easier it is to make choices about your future, both in your world of work and in your daily life.

In the church, career counseling involves more than just determining an appropriate career. Faith-based career counseling adds the dimension of seeking a meaningful life based on the belief that God created us and is calling us (1) to participate in the community that God intended creation to be and (2) to use our gifts in service to others. The goal of life and career is to move not inward but outward. The road to self-fulfillment is found in loving, caring, and serving. In other words, career counseling in the church assumes that people will not find meaningful life if all they are concerned about is themselves. Happiness is not found by pursuing "me first" or "me only" happiness. We are not created to be self-serving, consumed by our own needs, or as one writer put it, consumed by our own consuming.

This book is written for leaders, educators, ministers, and anyone else interested in developing a career

1

counseling ministry in the local church. The program is a small-group ministry designed for two populations: (1) high school juniors and seniors who are contemplating what they will do after graduation and (2) young adults who are in the midst of figuring out what they want to do in life. These young adults may include those who are in the career search process, those who already have jobs and want to explore other possibilities, and those who simply desire an opportunity to discern God's call and to discover a more meaningful life.

It is difficult to specify ages for these young adults. The sessions focus on God's call, who you are, and the world of work, and certainly, any age group could explore these areas. The program, however, is designed for people in the early stages of career search, rather than those whose main concern is career change.

This program invites young people and young adults on a journey to discover what God is calling them to be and do. It offers:

- connections between faith and work and between faith and lifestyle;
- a way to explore God's call—God calls us to a lifestyle and vocation;
- opportunities for relationships with adult leaders, mentors, friends, family, and significant adult friends in the church;
- a peer group, that is, a small group of participants and one or two adult leaders;
- activities for participants
    to know more about themselves, their interests, dreams, values, goals, personality styles, work styles, gifts, abilities;
    to look at the world of work;
    to invite God into the conversation about life and work.

This book is a guide for counselors, youth, and young adults. When we say "counselors," we mean any adult leader, lay or ordained, who leads youth or young adults through the career counseling program. This ministry does not require professional counselors. Leaders will need to read this book before beginning the sessions. Chapter 2 on God's call and chapter 3 on the practices of faith contain crucial information needed to discuss these subjects with the participants.

In chapter 1, "The Church's Unique Opportunity," we look at today's young people and young adults and their concerns about the future. We address the church's unique opportunity to offer faith-based career counseling.

Chapter 2 explores God's call, the idea that God calls people to a lifestyle as well as a career. God calls people to be who God created them to be. God's call is both to "be" and to "do."

Chapter 3 introduces practices of faith. To know God and to discern God's call, we must practice listening for God. We look at a few of the practices: prayer, meditation, journal writing, worship, sabbath, presence, and embodying.

Chapter 4 describes a design for career counseling ministry in the local church. The design uses the small-group model and includes six sessions, a journal, and a set of reproducible self-discovery forms. Extra sessions are highly recommended, as well as opportunities to develop mentor relationships, to make job site visits and college visits, and to involve parents, step-parents, or guardians.

Chapter 5 suggests ways in which parents or guardians can help, support, and become partners with their youth and young adult sons and daughters on the journey. Included is a session for parents and one for parents and career participants.

In chapter 6 we talk about mentors and offer guidelines for setting up mentor relationships. Chapter 7 discusses career counseling for young people and young adults with special needs, such as learning, mental, or physical disabilities.

Chapters 8 through 13 contain the six sessions of the career counseling program, two each on three topics: "God's Calling," "About You," and "The World of Work."

Chapter 14 suggests additional meetings of the group to remain in contact with one another and to continue activities and discussions begun during the six sessions, including informational interviews, job site visits, further education plans, summer activities, jobs, mentors, and progress on decision making. Included are eight additional scripture passages.

We also include three appendixes. The first contains a printed copy of the journal to photocopy for participants, as they will be writing in the journal both during and after the program. Participants who wish to keep their journals on their computers can log on to the Presbyterian Publishing Corp. Web site (www.ppcpub.com) and click on Download Materials. The second appendix is a design for a spirituality retreat. The third appendix is a list of resources, which includes a list of interdenominational counseling centers.

We offer in this book ideas and tools for establishing a career counseling ministry. Indeed, it is a ministry. We hope that in the context of talking about life, faith, the future, and decision making, those who participate in this ministry will deepen their relationships with God and discern how God is calling them in all aspects of their lives. Above all, our hope is that the church will be there for our youth and young adults at a critical time in their lives.

PART 1

CAREER COUNSELING MINISTRY

CHAPTER 1

The Church's Unique Opportunity

Of all the mirrors that help us establish identity, only the church allows us to see ourselves as God sees us: favored, beloved, blessed.[1]

What do you want to be when you grow up? Isn't it funny how such an innocent question, posed to a five-year-old who gleefully answers, "A fireman!" has a way of becoming the most haunting, gnawing question of a lifetime? It's a dilemma that many of us, no matter our age, are still trying to figure out. For today's teenagers and young adults, it tops the list of anxiety producers. What do I want to do with my life? So many people don't have a clue. They don't even know how to think about it.

> I think it hits most people during their junior year in high school, well, some not 'til senior year. All of a sudden, you've got to make a million decisions. Everybody's pressuring you—especially your parents. You're expected to know what you're going to do after graduation, what you're going to major in, in college. I don't even know if I want to go to college. It hits you like a ton of bricks. One day you're cruising along, then, bam, the questions start coming, and immediately you're full of regrets—should've taken different courses, should've studied more, should've cared about the SAT. Now I'm trying to apply to schools, which is a hassle when you don't know what you want to do. I'd like to find a job, but doing what? I just don't know.—Vince, a high school senior

Vince is not alone. These last two years of high school are decision time. What do I do after graduation? Will I go to college? What will I study? What career should I pursue? Can I get a job doing something I really enjoy? What will it be? How will I know? What's surprising is that these struggles are not limited to high school students. An enormous number of young adults wrestle with the same questions.

> I didn't know what I wanted to do when I was in high school. But I was sure that by the time I was twenty-one, I'd know. I'm twenty-four. I was a business major in college. I spent eight months looking for a job. Now I've got a job, but this is not "it," I mean it's not what I would call my career.—Denise, twenty-four

> The hardest part is when people ask you what you do. I'm unemployed right now. And I still don't know what I want to do. I worked at a refrigeration plant for two years after high school. Then I thought being a chef would be fun, so I went to cooking school. Definitely not me. Should I go to college? That would be four more years without significant income. I've got to find a job, but I don't want just any job. I'd like a career!—Sam, twenty-one

Not only are youth and young adults asking many of the same questions, but both groups face many of the same pressures as they seek to find their place in this world. Both are searching for the clues that will lead them to a meaningful life. Both are challenged by economics, family, relationships, and the world's standards of success and failure.

Many people today are interested in generational studies, and the church is benefiting from writers who interpret this information and offer implications for the community of faith. In this chapter, we look at the two generations that comprise our youth and young adults. We focus on each group separately, beginning with the young people, often called Millennials. We touch on characteristics and concerns of young people and then consider the church's unique opportunity to offer them career counseling ministry. We follow the same outline for young adults, most of whom are a part of the so-called Generation X. If you are interested in young adult ministry, you may skip down to your section, or you may read on and see how the two groups compare.

Two Generations: Generation X and Millennials

"It was the best of times, it was the worst of times." We are all familiar with this opening line from Charles Dickens's *A Tale of Two Cities*. Is the situation any different today? Not really. The turn of the century has provided us with as much reason for optimism as for despair. On the up side, opportunities for youth and young adults have never been more abundant. On the down side, communities, families, and churches struggle to cope with brokenness caused by abuse, greed, self-absorption, power lust, hatred, violence, and economic uncertainty. Today's youth and young adults are regularly described in contradictory terms: cynics and believers, self-indulgent and compassionate, remote and involved, scared and confident, stressed out and carefree. One thing is sure about "these times": they are not dull.

One explanation for the contradictions is that we are dealing with two generations. The first is the infamous Generation X, or baby busters (those born during 1965–1983[2] and so named because of the decline in birthrate after the baby boomers), whom researcher George Barna has called "world-class skeptics, cynical about mankind and pessimistic about the future. . . . Busters view education as a necessary evil. Their thrust is to gain whatever knowledge they must have to get by in life."[3]

The other generation, those born after 1983, are referred to as Millennials. One writer, Thom S. Rainer, has given them a more promising name, the Bridger Generation.[4] This generation is the bridge between centuries, and though we don't know as yet what kind of bridge they will be, that image brings to mind hope-filled images of connecting, overcoming obstacles, supporting, and joining.

If we use the year 2001 as a reference point, we find the first of the Millennials (eighteen-year-olds) entering the workforce, college, the military, or joining the unemployed. Those already in the workforce, military, and college are classified as Generation X. For our purposes as a church, beginning in 2001, youth ministry is with Millennials and young adult ministry is with Generation X, although, with each succeeding year, young adult ministry will include more Millennials. Now that we've done our labeling, we invite you to extract whatever insights are helpful from the following generalizations of the two generations, and then we ask you promptly to drop the labels and to be in ministry with God's beloved individuals of various ages.

Young People—Adolescents— Roughly Ages 13 to 19

Those of you in ministry with young people will be pleased and perhaps surprised with the results of studies of this generation. There is a resurgence of the values of family, faith, and compassion among today's teenagers, the so-called Millennials. This is a generation of hope-filled young people. They are spiritual, optimistic, and ambitious. I had the opportunity to talk with two female eighth graders from Paducah, Kentucky, a few years after the school shootings in which a fourteen-year-old killed three and wounded five stu- dents. These girls were very serious when they said that, when they grew up, they were going to do something about guns and violence, that their generation will make a difference. I believe them.

Family

In spite of being raised amid an environment of broken families, abuse, abandonment, negligible contact with parents and other adults, and economic uncertainty, this generation of young people expresses the desire to raise a family.[5] Whether positive or negative, parents are still the primary influence in their lives. According to the 1995 Barna research, "moms" top the list of persons teens turn to for reliable and useful guidance.[6] Teenagers spend an average of three and a half hours alone every day and "wished they had more adults in their lives, especially their parents."[7] We should not be surprised, then, that the number-one issue troubling adolescents is loneliness.

Parents of our young people need to hear this—that their teenage children want more time with them. If parents are assuming that their sons and daughters don't want them around, most likely they are wrong. Parents rarely recognize the powerful effect they have on their children.

Faith

The parents, stepparents, and guardians of this generation's teenagers are less involved with church and faith than any other generation and thus do not encourage their children to explore faith or to be a part of a church. Yet teenagers today are intensely interested in the spiritual, in one form or another. "Many teenagers believe that a major component of America's illness is that we have lost our sense of the divine and the mystical."[8] Fifty-one percent of teenagers spend two and a half hours each week going to religious functions.[9]

Compassion

Caring and altruism are important attributes to the Millennials. In increasing numbers, young people are serving in their communities, through high school, church, and community leadership and volunteer programs. Nearly two-thirds of all college undergraduates participate in volunteer activities.[10] In churches, young people frequently cite mission trips as their most significant faith experiences.

Concerns of Teenagers

Education tops the list of major concerns of teenagers. Young people are aware that the competition for both college admission and jobs is tough. They are under pressure from parents, teachers, coaches, and themselves to achieve. The top ten teenage concerns are:

education issues
relationships

emotional pressure
physical threats and violence
financial difficulties
substance abuse
morality and values
career considerations
health issues
religious issues or decisions[11]

It is interesting that career considerations fall in the latter half of the list. This makes sense when we consider that this study involved thirteen- to eighteen-year-olds. Since so many young people haven't a clue what they want to do, the career question often gets put on the back-burner until junior or senior year.

Developmental theorists identify the tasks of adolescence as being able to answer two questions: (1) Who am I? and (2) Where do I fit in this world?—the issues of identity and belonging. This task remains the same for each generation of adolescents, but the experiences along the journey to find answers can vary significantly from generation to generation. Today's young people have many more options and many more sources telling them what they should look like and be like than did previous generations. They experience an unprecedented level of stress and depression. The teenager is trying to find that niche, that paradoxical identity of being both a unique individual and one of the group, *some* group in which he or she can feel acceptance and belonging.

Studies show that, in comparison with former generations, today's teenagers are more serious about life and more resilient—they are surviving troubled home lives and economic uncertainties. Exposed to more information at a younger age and expected to fill adult roles in many homes, they are more savvy and often impatient with adults who don't take them seriously. They seek something deeper than what their world offers. The 1990s values of rationality, tolerance, and extreme individualism offer a cold isolation. No thanks; they already know what it's like to be lonely.

Church historian Martin Marty says, "Most youth are overwhelmed by the relativism that comes with postmodern observance. . . . Mere tolerance and mere indifference are not attitudes and expressions that will do justice to their dreams and passions."[12]

The Church's Unique Opportunity with Youth

What we have here is a picture of hope-filled young people. They are searching, and they care. What they are searching for can be found in one dependable, generous, and loving God, who is calling them to greater things than they can imagine. The challenge to the church is not to be wimpy about our mission and ministry. If the church does not model a faith that seeks justice, loves kindness, and walks humbly with God, if we Christians do not model lifestyles in which faith permeates our work, our relationships, and our daily living, then how can we expect young people to discern what God is calling them to be and do?

The church has a unique opportunity to invite young people on a journey of discovery and discernment. Career counseling ministry is designed to offer a safe place and a caring group where teenagers can explore issues, shape and reshape dreams, and discover their passions with adults who take them seriously and who will listen. The career counseling program exposes them to and invites them into communities that model faith for them.

Perhaps it's time for the cynics among us who assume that youth don't care about anything, that they are put off by church and spiritual things, to take a new look at these young people. We will see individuals hungering for truth, seeking God but not sure how to connect, and yearning for adults who would walk with them on a path toward a significant life that matters, an abundant life that makes a difference.

Young Adults—Roughly Ages 19 to 35

In many cases this age could be described as a time of prolonged adolescence. That is a phenomenon and paradox of our times, which is evidenced by several factors. First, more young adults than ever before are living at home, mostly out of economic necessity— after graduation from high school, after college, after divorce, often returning home with babies. It's hard not to feel like an adolescent when you're living with a parent.

Second, as we noted above, the tasks of adolescence are identity and belonging. These days, especially, the identity question is not settled when a person turns eighteen. Young adults are still trying to find out who they are and where they fit in this world. Many in this age group do not know any more about their vocational direction than they did in high school.

Third, this generation has been characterized as the "postponing generation."[13] They put off making decisions as long as possible. In light of economic uncertainty, job competition, and the many available options, they are afraid of making wrong choices. And they are conscious of how the culture ties self-worth to performance. You are what you do.

This generation has been viewed as a casualty of the 1970's Me Generation. They inherited a world messed up by their parents, a world of drugs, divorce, and drained resources. They were the first generation of which it could not be said, "They'll be better off than their parents." So a major concern of the so-called Generation X is that they will never have enough money. As a result, practicality and skepticism define their approach to life. They are either pessimistic or ambivalent about the future.

As with adolescents, stress and pressure are issues.

But the condition is worse. Young adults are older and feel they should have their act together but don't. They feel the pressure of other people's expectations. The internal pressure is heightened. Young adults are hard on themselves.

The distinctive developmental task of young adults is intimacy. Relationships are important at this stage of life. Young adults want and need close friendships. They need someone with whom they can share themselves, as we used to say, "warts and all." Yet they are also afraid of commitment, for they have seen the ravages of wars over divorce and the dissolution of families.

They live fast-paced lives. They often feel alienated from family, community, and God. They are spiritual, but not in the traditional sense. Spirituality is variously defined in our culture—from New Age, yoga, scientology, and cults to relativism, where all beliefs are accepted. All of this reflects a search for meaning that flits from one interest or focus to another. Many young adults don't know what they want.

Concerns of Young Adults

According to researcher George Barna, the personal issues baby busters consider to be most significant are:

    personal financial problems
    career/job pressures, challenges
    completion/furthering of education
    family-related challenges
    relationships and social difficulties
    coping with substance abuse

overcoming transportation problems
handling time pressures
fear of crime[14]

These concerns should not surprise us. Finances and career are right at the top. The Barna researchers go on to say, "The life conditions deemed considerably more desirable by Busters than by older adults are having close friendships with people; having a high-paying job; exerting influence in the lives of other people; owning a large home; achieving some measure of fame or public recognition; and living comfortably."[15]

The paradoxes of this generation are interesting. They crave intimacy but not commitment. They want a carefree life, yet they also want responsibility and power. They want mobility but also roots. They want the upscale lifestyle but can't afford it.

The Church's Unique Opportunity with Young Adults

The young adult situation may seem bleak to some. But this is all the more reason for churches to focus on young adult ministry. Too many churches ignore this age group, for the various subgroups—college students away, college students in town, singles, married couples, those married with children, the divorced, single parents—are so diverse that ministry with this age group can be difficult. So the church chooses to leave them alone, hoping that when they settle down, they will come back to the fold. Unfortunately, the theory that young adults leave the church and come back when they have children lost credibility a couple decades ago.

Young adult ministry is critical, for young adults are facing the big decisions about life and are going through transitions of location, dwelling, friends, employers; they are scared and desperately need the church, and we must be there. Many ministers and church leaders recognize this. In a young adult ministry newsletter, Handt Hanson, a Lutheran worship team leader, wrote, "This generation carries a great deal of emotional pain and if we intend to minister to this group, we need to learn about their pain. We need to understand how they view the world. Most importantly, we need to demonstrate authentic, honest love. Over and over, this generation is inviting the church to 'get to know me.'"[16]

The church has a unique opportunity, through career counseling ministry, to offer a safe place, a concerned group, and a caring environment where young adults are accepted as people of infinite worth simply because they are God's own. Career ministry invites them to new ways of seeing themselves, their lives, and their vocations, of discovering what's important to them, and it offers appropriate resources. With a group of peers and leaders who will join them on a journey of inviting God into the conversation, they can discover a God who transforms, a faith that works, and a lifestyle of responding to God's call.

As we said in the discussion on youth, what young adults are searching for can be found in one dependable, generous, and loving God who is calling them to greater things than they can imagine. We in the church have a ministry here—to model a lifestyle and faith style that cares about others more than self; that is concerned about suffering and injustice; that exemplifies gratitude, generosity, and grace; and that loves generously because of God's generous love for us. We are called by God to model this lifestyle in all that we do, in our work, our relationships, and our daily living. The career counseling program invites young adults to experience and become a part of this community of faith.

Why the Church?

If I were looking for career counseling, why wouldn't I go to a high school or college counselor or a professional career counselor, or just take some tests on the Internet? This is a frequently asked and commonsense question.

Good career counseling services are available in the secular arena. We recommend that youth and young adults use as many resources as possible. Many colleges and universities are increasing their career development staff to serve more students. On the high school level, however, even though many schools have good counselors, the student-counselor ratio usually prohibits offering individual students a significant amount of time.

There are also career counseling sites on the Internet, as well as career guidance software, such as SIGI Plus, that helps people systematically examine how work-related values, interests, and skills match up with occupational options. It points to duties, educational requirements, and other details about prospective careers.

At counseling centers, clients are given personal inventories or instruments, such as the Strong Vocational,

Emotional Intelligence, and Myers-Briggs Type Indicator. Based on test results and consultation, the counselor helps clients see patterns in their interests, preferences, and skills and points them to possible career fields to consider. The clients may also receive guidance regarding steps to take, education possibilities, information on specific careers, and personal skills to develop.

Some career centers and counselors specialize in the job search process, so it's important to investigate and see if the center or counselor is offering the kinds of services that are needed. Many of the centers are quite expensive.

We strongly support the use of interdenominational career development centers, which see themselves as a ministry. They provide the strongest partnership with this book's career counseling program, since they are faith based. Because the centers are a ministry, their services are less expensive than those of secular counselors. If you are located near an interdenominational career center, you are fortunate. Take full advantage of its services. If you are not, your church would benefit from offering a retreat or road trip to a center in conjunction with this program. (See appendix 3 for a listing of interdenominational centers.)

What the Church Has to Offer

Since people are often pessimistic or cynical about the role of the church in a secular society, the words of Princeton educators Ron Foster and Kenda Creasy Dean are reassuring: "In a world increasingly defined by virtual reality, the church remains a harbinger of authentic relationships and primary experience."[17]

The church is in a unique position to offer faith-based career counseling, to approach career guidance as a ministry, to connect a youth or young adult's search for career with that individual's search for meaning in life as a child of God. The church can offer eight distinctive benefits.

1. *A ministry that is ongoing, connected, and relational:* Secular career counseling is usually a one-time event, one or two days of testing and counseling. Centers and counselors offer a positive service, for clients usually take away helpful insights and good advice. At the same time, career counseling is an isolating endeavor in its one-on-one or one-on-computer approach.

The church, by contrast, approaches career counseling as a ministry, as one of the many ministries of the local church. Therefore, it is intended to be ongoing, relational, and connected to the life of the church. The career counseling program we present in this book promotes significant relationships with caring leaders and mentors from the congregation, relationships that can continue over months and years.

2. *A care group/support group of fellow sojourners:* The journey to discover what God is calling us to be and do is greatly enhanced when it is experienced with a caring, supportive group of partners on the journey. We learn more about God and about ourselves as we listen to others' reflections and views. Other people's perspectives help shape and reshape our thinking.

3. *The resource of congregations full of people who have a common identity, commitment, and value sys-*

tem: The community of faith gathers around one Lord and shares a common lifestyle of responding to the call of God in Jesus Christ. What a wonderful resource for youth and young adults who are beginning the journey, who are struggling to find meaning and direction in life! In the congregation are models of mature faith and fellow sojourners seeking to be faithful. In the congregation are people who care, who are willing to share their life experiences. In the congregation are mentors, significant adult friends, and potential contacts in the work world. The church is a great place to start networking.

4. *The integration of faith and work, faith and lifestyle:* The church ministers to the whole person, not just the soul or a person's beliefs. The church claims that all of life is to be lived in response to God's call, that our work and life, our careers and lifestyle, all our activities and relationships are directly connected to the abundant love and creative work of our generous God. There is no separation between faith and work or between faith and lifestyle. This affirmation gives greater depth to the career search process.

5. *The perception of self as co-creator with God:* The striking difference between secular career counseling and faith-based counseling is in the basic assumptions. Career counseling ministry claims a distinctive definition of self as created in the image of God for the purposes of God. As God's own, we, in a sense, are co-creators with God. God gives us gifts with which to continue the creative process God has begun. We are partners with God in ministry and mission, in loving, serving, caring, doing justice, and calling the world to do the same.

6. *Confidence in the unconditional, enduring love and care of God:* Knowing who we are and our place in God's world gives us a unique confidence. We may be unsure of our abilities and not know what our next

step will be, but we are confident that the uncondi-tional, enduring love of our Creator is taking care of us. We are confident that God is present with us, guiding us, and cheering us on. We know God delights in us and wants us to be about our callings, discovering who we are, where we belong, and what roles we are to play in life.

7. *Ways to invite God into the conversation of career and lifestyle:* A young college professor pushed the issue of God's call. He said, "I'm very happy with my career. I feel good about the way I came to the decision to teach. I like the way my career path devel-oped. Why would I need or want to consider what God is calling me to do?" It hadn't occurred to him that per-haps he was doing exactly what God was calling him to do. Just because he wasn't aware of God's presence on his career path didn't mean that God was not involved. He either hadn't noticed or hadn't made the connection.

Career counseling ministry is not just for those who are frustrated or clueless as to what they ought to be doing in life. On the contrary, many who participate in the career sessions know exactly what they want to do, and some are already doing it. But they want more. They seek a deeper meaning to life. In the process of discovering ways to listen for God, they learn to trust that they are doing what God has called them to do. They recognize that God created them with the talents they're using. What's different is the way their work and their exploration take on new energy, creativity, and passion. They begin to sense God's presence not only in their vocation but in all of life. Their goals, intentions, and actions reflect a healthier sense of who they are, the beloved of God, in whom God delights. They discover a more abundant life, which is what God wanted for them in the first place.

The church offers opportunities for individuals to explore together ways of inviting God into the conver-sation of career and lifestyle choices and decisions. In chapter 3 we discuss several practices of faith that teach participants how to listen for God and to practice integrating faith with work and lifestyle.

8. *The assurance that you can't make a mistake:* It may seem unrealistic to say, "You can't make a mis-take." Of course, you can make mistakes and should

expect to do so. But often people are filled with regret and despair over "wrong" choices. They regret choos-ing the wrong college or accepting the wrong job offer. The effects of such regret can be devastating—a sense of not being able to make it in this world, of perceiv-ing oneself as a failure; a feeling of losing ground instead of progressing on a career path. This loss of confidence can lead to a paralyzing fear of making choices.

Young people can be easily discouraged and pre-sume that choosing the wrong college or career field can ruin their futures. We have encountered many who speak of "wasting a whole year" at the "wrong" col-lege. To them, it's a huge mistake. For this reason we suggest a new way of thinking about mistakes. We decided to make the statement "You can't make a mis-take" a key concept of career counseling ministry. The church is in a unique position to support young people and young adults and to assure them that they cannot make a mistake.

Spending a miserable year at the wrong college or wrong job is not a mistake. Tremendous life skills are learned in such a situation—coping skills, conflict management, courage, stamina, determination, new understandings about life, vocation, self, and God. Often, though, people are in such despair over the per-ceived mistake, the wrong choice, that they cannot see the value of the experience. We want those going through career counseling ministry not to let failure or mistakes dominate their lives and destroy their spirits. We invite them to view failures and mistakes as God-given opportunities to grow and learn.

Of course, we fail; we sin; we make poor decisions. Failures can bring us closer to God, as we acknowl-edge that we can't make everything right, and that we cannot succeed if our only resource is ourselves. We acknowledge our need for God and recognize that God will not abandon us. God loves us through our failures. We recognize that there is meaning and pur-pose in the disasters and disappointments of life.

What seems a hindrance becomes a way;
what seems like an obstacle becomes a door;
what seems a misfit becomes a cornerstone.[18]
Henri Nouwen

Closing

In career counseling ministry, youth and young adults encounter adult leaders who are also in the midst of discerning God's call in their own lives. At First Presbyterian Church in Dalton, Georgia, Nancy

and Rob have led our career counseling groups for over five years. They both saw career counseling min-istry as part of their calls. Ironically, both of them were fired from previous jobs in the same year. Instead of being devastated, however, they trusted that the next step in their calls would become clear.

Nancy realized that she needed to be on a new venture to discover what God was calling her to do next. Her involvement in the church on weekends was an important part of her life and calling, and it had been increasingly hard for her to keep doing a job where she had to put her personal ethics on the shelf during the week. She was relieved to have the chance to move on.

Rob was discouraged at first. Citing his trust in God's providence, however, he began to view his firing as merely the closing of one door. He knew another would open. As it turned out, door closings have led him to change careers from law enforcement to sales to teaching. He has grown in his understanding of the many ways in which God has called him and will continue to call him.

Our church has been grateful that these faith-filled leaders were willing to share these experiences with our career participants. What wonderful role models! They modeled confidence and faith in God's enduring love and care. The church is indeed a unique place where adult leaders and youth and young adults can share in the search to listen for God, discern God's call, and explore the exciting world of career and calling.

CHAPTER 2

God's Call

We are created in the image of God for the purpose of God.

"If I were to ask you, 'What do you feel God is calling you to be and do?' how would you answer that question?" That's the question we've been asking people for the last four years. We have heard a variety of answers:

> "I feel God is calling me to be in service to people in some way. I'm interested in teaching English in a Hispanic country."
>
> "I think—but I'm not sure—but right now I think God wants me to work with little kids in some way."
>
> "I believe I'm doing what I'm called to do because I can fail so often and still keep doing it and still be happy doing it."
>
> "To be a supportive wife and good mother."
>
> "To be a performer and a person who expresses lots of stuff to reach and bring joy to others."
>
> "To make this world a better place."
>
> "To make a difference."
>
> "I have no idea."
>
> "Do you mean in my job or in my life?"
>
> "I believe in God, but that's just my belief. I work as a consultant in marketing."

It's a fascinating experiment, bringing God into the conversation with this question, especially with people you haven't known for more than a few minutes, like the person sitting next to you on a plane. Some of the people are baffled; others have no notion of an incarnate God, involved in people's lives. For many, it was a question they very much wanted to discuss. The conversations gave us an idea of the struggles people have with faith and life and reassured us that this book needed to be written.

Although there are no right or wrong answers, every once in a while we would hear an answer that was right on target—"on target" meaning that these persons had an evolving understanding of God at work in their lives and a healthy relationship with their Creator. This was the case with a young man, twenty-five years old, who had graduated from college with a degree in business, having first majored in pre-med, then in biology. As part of a high school mentor program, he had worked in an ophthalmologist's office. He spent the first year after college graduation working two jobs, one in hospital administration, the other as a substitute middle school teacher. Both hospital and school administrators were prepared to offer him full-time jobs. In the summer of that first year, he worked as our interim director of youth ministry, after which the senior pastor and I both encouraged him to consider youth ministry as a career. He had, however, just been accepted in an MBA program.

With great interest, I asked him *the* question, "What do you feel God is calling you to be and do?" expecting that he would be totally confused about his life. Well, he brightened and said, "I know exactly what God is calling me to be and do." That certainly got my attention. He said, "God is calling me to figure out what I'm supposed to do with my life." He was serious. He was not anxious. He saw all the dabbling in career fields as God's way of leading him to what he should do first.

What a wonderful answer! He is right where so many young adults are—not sure about their future but continuing to try to figure out what to do with their lives. This young man, however, is where we'd like to see all youth and young adults. He is aware that God is calling him to a process of learning more about himself, careers, and God. He is confident of God's love for him and that God will reveal the steps he needs to take to be faithful in life and work.

That's the purpose of this book—to help people

answer the question "What is God calling me to do first? or next?" But before we can answer that question, we have to figure out what God's call is. What does "call" mean? And how do we find out what that call is? Let's first look at some misconceptions about God's call.

Misconception #1: God's Call Refers Only to Church Professions

Many people think that when we talk about people hearing God's call, we are referring only to those people who have heard God's call to become ministers, preachers, church educators, evangelists, missionaries, all those "church" professions. They may know that in the organization of the church, the term *call* refers to what happens to people when they perceive God's will as directing them into ordained or nonordained ministry or other church-related professions. The term is also used to describe the actual hiring of ministers: for instance, a church issues a call to someone to serve as its pastor. It's not unusual to hear pastors talk about their next "call" rather than their next "job."

The Real Story: God's call is for everyone, in all walks of life, in all professions, in all circumstances. God calls plumbers, technicians, stockbrokers, managers, florists, garbage collectors, engineers, grocery clerks, movie stars, football players, editors, therapists, teachers, Internet servicers, caregivers, volunteers, moms, dads, children, encouragers, mentors. Notice how the list moved from paid professions to other forms of vocation. A seven-year-old girl is called to be child, daughter, niece, student, friend, and play specialist.

Misconception #2: There Is Only One Call of God for Each Person

When asked the question, "What is God calling you to be and do?" several people implied that God's call is to one vocation in life, and that your task is to discover that one thing. If you have had a string of jobs or multiple careers, they are only preliminary stops along the way to finding what God *really* wants you to do.

The Real Story: There is not just one thing people are meant to do in life. There is not just one call of God. God calls us to a variety of roles, activities, and jobs, in which God continues to call us to serve in many ways. This does not discredit those who report that they have found their calling in a particular voca-

tion. Nor does it make light of the yearning, the passion, the "something gnawing at you," as one person described it, that people reported as leading them to recognize one particular vocation to which God was calling them. There is, however, the possibility that God may call these people to move in another direction at a later time. They may also sense God's call in other areas of their lives.

The liberating news in all this is that a person does not have to make one career decision for life. Young people and young adults need to hear that they do not have to decide now what they want to do for the rest of their lives. Rather, they need to focus on what they want to do first. What is God calling you to be and do first?

Misconception #3: God Calls Other People, But Not Me

Some people think that God's call is to other people, special people, those who are more religious or closer to God or those who are nicer, kinder, and more loving than I am. God sees something in other people that God can use, but not in me. I am not worthy to be included in that special group of people who are called by God.

The Real Story: This misconception could be related to the first, that God's call is only to church professions. In any case, it comes from a sense of inferiority and a misunderstanding of who God is. The view that God calls only those who are religious, kind, and loving reflects poor theology. It's theology based on a kind of works righteousness—that people need to shape up, do good, and work harder in order to be loved, or even noticed, by God. It's hard for many people to hear, really hear, that God does indeed love them, and they don't have to do anything to earn that love.

God's call is to everyone. God calls us (all of us) because God loves us (all of us) so much. From the creation story we learn that God, not wanting to be alone, created us humans, the masterpiece of creation, to live in relationship with God. God created us in God's own image, so that we might reflect God's love and goodness. In giving us dominion over the earth, God gave us work to do. *Everyone* is called to continue God's work in some way.

In the Sacrament of Baptism we celebrate and affirm the love God has for us. In baptism we are claimed by God and called by God to ministry and service. It is in our baptism that we receive our vocation to be a part

> "We love because he first loved us."
> 1 John 4:19

of God's great work on earth. If we look at the sequence of events at Jesus' baptism (Luke 3:21–23), we discover how Jesus received his call to ministry. At his baptism, the Holy Spirit descended on Jesus, and a voice from heaven claimed him: "You are my Son, the Beloved; with you I am well pleased." At the age of thirty, Jesus began his work with a forty-day retreat into the wilderness, led by the Spirit, for some serious reflection time, preparation, and temptation. In Luke 4 we see that Jesus, filled with the power of the Spirit, began the teaching part of his vocation by stating his call: "to bring good news to the poor . . . to proclaim release to the captives and recovery of sight to the blind, to let the oppressed go free, to proclaim the year of the Lord's favor" (Luke 4:18–19).

With Jesus' process of call as our model, we learn that we, too, are God's beloved. God claims us, has given us work to do, and will be with us through the power of the Spirit. From Jesus' call, and from the entire message of the Bible, we learn that God calls us to a radically new way of being human, to an alternate way of running the world, much different from the way our culture teaches.

Misconception #4: Certain Vocations Are More Pleasing to God than Others; for That Matter, Certain People Are More Pleasing to God than Others

If asked, "Does God play favorites?" many people would say yes. Since there are so many "bad" people in the world, surely God is more pleased with some than others. Likewise, God must be pleased with some people's choices of vocation and not others'. If Don works for a meat-packaging company, and Dan works for the Red Cross, well, surely God is more pleased with Dan than with Don, because Dan spends his time helping others, while Don just cuts up meat.

The Real Story: To think that God would be more pleased with Dan than with Don suggests that God has a rated listing, a ranking order, of God-pleasing professions. That presents a very narrow, humanly skewed view of God. The God we know from the Old and New Testaments does not work that way. This misconception likely comes from the same sense of inferiority or the same bad theology as the previous misconception.

God delights in us, each and every one of us. *Every* person is a creation of God. *Every* person is created in the image of God for the purposes of God. Our job, as created ones, whether we are meatpackers or Red Cross workers, is to discover what God would have us do in our lives both on the job and off the job.

We are not saying that every job is pleasing to God. Surely, God does not call people to be hit men, prostitutes, or extortionists. Yet we must be cautious here, for it is not our place to draw up a list of God-pleasing professions and those that are not God-pleasing. Where would we draw the line? And how would we judge? No, that is God's call, not ours.

Surely we can say that if a job requires a person to work against God's purposes, it is not God-pleasing. But how do we know if we are working against God's purposes? That question is addressed in this career ministry program as we seek to discern what God is calling us to be and do. We are called to discern whether we can be faithful in each and every occupation.

Misconception #5: One's Relationship to God Is a Private Matter, to Be Lived Out at Church, at Home, but Rarely at Work

The world abounds with people who consider their beliefs a private matter. Relationship with God may be talked about at church and at home but not at work. Our culture encourages such privacy. It also promotes a compartmentalization of our lives. We have our work life, our home life, our church life, not to mention a whole mess of extracurricular lives. Faith, therefore, would be slotted for church life. Furthermore, the term *faith* commonly refers to a belief system, not a way of life.

The Real Story: First of all, faith is personal, yes, but it is not private. Growing in faith requires community. God calls us together as the church and calls us out into the world to serve. We need the support and nurturing of the community of faith to follow that call. The Christian faith is not a privatized faith. It is a way of life that is communal and relational, both in essence and in mission.

Second, it is difficult for many people to grasp the concept of vocation, of connecting God and God's will with how we make money. Money enables us to survive and, for many, to provide for a family. It's a necessity. But we have ingrained in us the idea that money and God are at opposite poles, two different worlds. So we're in a dilemma: we have to have money, but it's the "root of evil." Thus we say, "Let's just not think about God in the work half of our being."

To compartmentalize life and live for God only on Sundays or only in private lives at home is to miss out on the wonderful way God intended it to be. Those who seek God's call for a part-time venture will have a hard time discerning that call, because they limit the compartments of their lives that God can enter. No part of our lives is hidden from God, and we should recognize that God can use every part in guiding us into God's future and our future. We must live all of life, not just part of it, in response to God's call. We are created by God to fulfill God's purposes here on earth. God chose us. God delights in us. God wants to be in relationship with us in all aspects of our lives. This is good news.

Somewhere we got the idea that talking about faith was taboo. If faith is such an important part of who we are, shouldn't we be talking about it? The problem is many of us don't know how. We need practice. We need a community of fellow sojourners who can help us practice.

What Is God's Call?

What exactly is God's call? First of all, God's call is an invitation to be in relationship with God. The term *call* implies a caller. God makes the call. It also implies a receiver, the person who hears the call and answers. Hearing a call takes discernment. This is challenging, for discernment requires listening and making decisions. But the relationship between the lover—God—and the beloved—us—makes discernment not only possible but a desirable part of our growth in faith. God's call gives life meaning and purpose. An important part of daily living, then, is listening for God.

God's call is also God's bidding us to follow Jesus Christ and to fulfill God's mission and purpose in the world. The invitation is reminiscent of Jesus' calling the brothers Simon (Peter) and Andrew, as they were busy with their careers as fishermen, with the simple invitation to "follow me." He identified their call by saying, "I will make you fish for people."

God's call is God's invitation and beckoning to us to be who God wants us to be and to do what God wants us to do. God calls us to vocation, to specific tasks both in the work world and outside the work world. Within these vocations, God calls us to various attitudes and activities that push us beyond ourselves toward service to and care for others. In these vocations we are called to fulfill God's mission and purpose.

God's call is God's specific way of relating to each one of us. Our call is that which connects us to God. God's call is the realization that God is actually talking to *you*. Perhaps it can best be described as the vital presence of God within us that moves us in a certain direction.

We speak of "hearing" God's call. Is it a voice? We speak of discerning God's call. Is it intuition? There is no one way to describe how people hear God's call. Some people explain their discernment of God's call as "nudges." They have felt God nudging them to do something. Others have sensed it as a result of living in the presence of God and participating in spiritual disciplines or practices of faith. (We discuss this in chapter 3.)

The We-ness of God's Call

A critical factor in our successfully discerning God's call is the affirmation of the call by those who know us well. Seminary professor and Christian educator Rodger Nishioka speaks of the "we-ness" of the call. The process of God's call involves more than just "me and God." God is community oriented and works in and through the community when calling. Some people tell of a teacher, pastor, friend, or colleague to whom they credit a career move. They cite these people as instruments of God's call.

For instance, suppose you felt God was calling you to be a sports agent. You would talk to friends, family, and significant adult friends in the church. They can validate the gifts and skills you feel you have for the job. They can raise questions you haven't considered. They can point out ways God might use you to achieve God's purposes in a profession often known for its greed. You could end up influencing a rising-star athlete to pursue a lifestyle of generosity and service.

By contrast, these friends might raise issues of concern. They might question your motivation. Their concerns need not throw you off course or destroy your dream. In fact, confronting such challenges may clarify your vision and strengthen your resolve to pursue the career. Or the dialogue might lead you to question whether God is calling you to be a sports agent.

That's why we suggest that you participate in a career counseling group. We do not recommend taking the sessions and doing the exercises at home alone. We believe God uses other people to bring to light our gifts, our personality styles, even our interests. People see things about us that we can't see. Therefore, other people are an essential part of the process of God's call.

God's Call Is Ongoing

God's call is not a once-and-for-all beckoning to one activity, career, or role in life. Rather, God's call is ongoing. True, some people feel called to just one career, but many find that God has called them to move in "a different direction" at various points in their lives. Career change is a cultural phenomenon we have carried into the twenty-first century. No longer do we stay in the same business for life. The young man who all his life planned to work in his family's publishing business has instead, by the age of thirty, changed careers four times. Even within a career field, many people sense that God is calling them to change jobs and move in new directions.

There is not just one thing that God calls us to be and do. As we listen for God and seek to discern God's call, we find that the call of God relates to more than careers and occupations. God calls us to certain tasks and roles in family life, extracurricular activities, relationships, and church. God calls us to play all these roles, all at the same time. Yet within these roles God calls us to new ventures, new activities, and new attitudes. We find that God's call is closely associated with our passions, gifts, talents, and abilities.

Given this understanding of God's call, we can create a lengthy list of what God is calling us to be and do. In one week God may call us to listen to a hurting friend, to write a note, to speak out about an issue, to teach, to soothe, or to care. Because God's call is ongoing, Christians continue to listen for God in all aspects of daily life.

God Calls Us to a Lifestyle and a Vocation

What do we mean when we say that God's call involves more than a person's job or profession? We mean that God's call is to a lifestyle and a vocation. By lifestyle, we are referring to how people choose to live their lives. This includes values, commitments, family, friends, church involvement, volunteer activities, work, play, rest, all the ways in which people use their time.

By vocation, we refer to professions, occupations, and jobs, but we take it a step further. The word *vocation* comes from the Latin word *vocare,* "to call." Your vocation is your calling. It's what God is calling you to be and do. Your vocation is that particular activity to which you perceive God is calling you. And it could be an activity for which you are not paid. As an example, a dental assistant says her vocation is clowning. As a volunteer clown, she visits children in hospitals and teaches clowning to teenagers and adults. A postal employee says God has called him to youth and college ministry, also as a volunteer. Both the dental assistant and postal employee admit that God does call them in their paid jobs, but they regard their volunteer roles as a calling. Volunteer activities are vocations for many men and women. Being a parent is a vocation. Being a caregiver is a vocation.

God *does* call us to work. We are created to continue God's creative process by replenishing the earth and taking care of it (Genesis 1:28; 2:15):

> God has created the world for a purpose. In the divine economy, human beings made in the image of God uniquely participate in the fulfillment of that divine intention. In all the vicissitudes of life, the only worthy goal is the will of God.[1]

The good news is that we don't have to do this work alone. We are to stay in conversation with God, to partner with God in carrying out God's intentions. Throughout the Bible, we see that God intends for the created ones to be in a continuing dialogue and relationship with God and to be in community with others.

So what are we supposed to do? If God calls us to a lifestyle and a vocation, how do we live? We find the answer in the life and teachings of Jesus. Jesus stated it quite simply, "Come, follow me." What Jesus called the disciples to, what God calls us to, is a way of living. Our call is to follow Jesus, to continue his work on earth. This call involves the whole of our being, not just our jobs. It involves family, education, leisure, church, and volunteer activities. The call to follow Christ is a call to a lifestyle and a vocation. The two are intertwined.

Throughout the New Testament we find clues as to what this lifestyle might include. Jesus called the disciples to a lifestyle of loving, caring service, as exemplified in Christ's own life and teachings—a lifestyle of declaring God's wonderful deeds (1 Peter 2:9–10); a lifestyle of loving God and neighbor (Matthew 22:37–39). Look at the Sermon on the Mount (Matthew 5–7). Look at the twelfth chapter of Paul's letter to the Romans, verses 9–21:

> Paul writes: "I . . . beg you to lead a life worthy of the calling to which you have been called." Ephesians 4:1

> Let love be genuine; hate what is evil, hold fast to what is good; love one another with mutual affection; outdo one another in showing honor. Do not lag in zeal, be ardent in spirit, serve the Lord. Rejoice in hope, be patient in suffering, persevere in prayer. Contribute to the needs of the saints; extend hospitality to strangers.

> Bless those who persecute you; bless and do not curse them. Rejoice with those who rejoice, weep with those who weep. Live in harmony with one another; do not be haughty, but associate with the lowly; do not claim to be wiser than you are. Do not repay anyone evil for evil, but take thought for what is noble in the sight of all. If it is possible, so far as it depends on you, live peaceably with all. Beloved, never avenge yourselves, but leave room for the wrath of God; for it is written, "Vengeance is mine, I will repay, says the Lord." No, "if your enemies are hungry, feed them; if they are thirsty, give them something to drink; for by doing this you will heap burning coals on their heads." Do not be overcome by evil, but overcome evil with good.

Each phrase of this passage is rich. Each verse could serve as the focus for meditation.

Or look at Galatians 5:22. There we find a list of lifestyle characteristics, called the "fruit of the Spirit." From this list we discover that God calls us to a lifestyle of love, joy, peace, patience, kindness, goodness, faithfulness, gentleness, and self-control. If we want to discover what kind of life God is calling us to live, meditating on each of the nine fruits of the Spirit is not a bad place to start.

God Calls Us to a Lifestyle of Gratitude

As we discussed in chapter 1, figuring out what to do with their lives is the dilemma facing older adolescents and young adults. As they listen for God and seek to discern God's will, they must make decisions. Scriptural guidelines, such as the fruits of the spirit, are helpful; but even with these, they still have decisions to make and questions to answer: How will I be faithful? To whom will I show kindness? How will I demonstrate patience? How will I work for peace?

So many decisions. We want to accept the challenge of living a life of faithfulness to God, of living as God would have us live, but it seems so overwhelming. What is wonderful about the faithfulness of God is that at the times when we are at our low points, God reaches us with "aha" moments, little glimpses of truth, small breakthroughs in our understanding of what's going on.

As a writer, I find it's these "ahas" that keep me going. It was during a time of struggling with this whole arena of God's call and at the same time enjoying a new and liberating understanding of God's grace that I experienced an "aha" in answer to the question: To what does God call us? The answer was gratitude. This is not a new concept. Much has been written about gratitude. In 1996, *The Simple Abundance Journal of Gratitude,* by Sarah Ban Breathnach, became a best-seller. In the journal, people were to write five things each day for which they were grateful. It encouraged people to make a habit of recognizing blessings daily. Many of us are not tuned in to blessings. We are more likely to be aware of what goes wrong in a day than of the "gifts" we are given.

As part of this "aha," I happened to read 1 Thessalonians 5:18 (NIV), "give thanks in all circumstances, for this is God's will for you in Christ." It became quite clear that God calls us to a lifestyle of gratitude. What was exciting to me was that gratitude does not require the decision making that other aspects of our lives require. Granted, it may not be easy to live gratefully, but the decisions regarding "who" and "what" have already been made. God is the who, and "all circumstances" is the what. We are grateful to God in all circumstances. What we are to do, then, is raise our awareness of the good gifts that God has given us, even those that may not seem good at the time—and give thanks.

Gratitude is a lifestyle. It also is a practice of faith, which we discuss in the next chapter. As we practice gratitude, we make space for God, because our focus shifts away from ourselves and toward God. When we practice gratitude, we "hear" God better. It becomes easier to listen for God, to be in conversation with God, when we are in a state of, or lifestyle of, gratitude. Practicing gratitude, making gratitude a habit, is life changing. It changes our attitudes and our dispositions. It changes the way we look at life. It is God's will that we give thanks in all circumstances.

God Calls Us to Be

We live in a culture that puts too much emphasis on what a person does. The problem with this is it implies that one's value as a person is directly related to one's occupation. When we meet people, our first question is usually "What do you do?" It's hard not to be evaluative when we hear the answer. Think how many times you thought, "How exciting" or "She really must be important" or "He must not be very smart." Consider how an unemployed person must feel when asked that question. (My husband has found a solution. Instead of asking, "What do you do?" he says, "Tell me about yourself," which frees people to answer in any way they choose.) We shouldn't, but we often do assign worth to another based on what a person does. Similarly, people judge or evaluate themselves based on what they do.

But our worth should come solely from our identity as children of God, created in the image of God. God calls us to be who we were created to be—people of infinite worth. I will always remember my dad, who was accustomed to a high level of respect—he was a judge—for a particular phrase he used when encouraging my mother and me to seek a special favor. "Tell them who you are," he would say, and my mother would grumble, "And who are we?"

Years later, that question continues to cause me to reflect. Who are we? Indeed, we are something special, because of God's claim on us and God's love for us. "Hey, I'm a child of God" is what I should have said in response to my mother's query. If you think about it, there is no better answer to the identity question.

Who are we? We "are a chosen people, a royal priesthood, a holy nation, a people belonging to God, that (we) may declare the praises of him who called (us) out of the darkness into his wonderful light. Once (we) were not a people, but now (we) are the people of God" (1 Peter 2:9–10 NIV).

So we speak of the call of God in terms of what God is calling us to be and do. We should be encouraging young people and young adults to think not just about what they are to do with their lives but also about who they are to be. We should offer them time and a place to reflect, to ask themselves:

> What kind of person is God calling me to be?
> How does God want me to live my life?
> What should I care about?

These are the questions they should be asking, rather than "What am I to do?"

God Calls Us to Be Faithful

In career counseling, we point young people and young adults to the truth about themselves—that they are the prized work of the Creator. We invite them on a journey to discover their gifts and interests and to explore the vocations in which their God-given talents might flourish.

If that were all we did for our youth and young adults, however, it would be a disservice. The destination of the journey is not to find the career for which they are best suited. That would be self-serving. Rather, the destination of the journey is faithfulness. God calls us to be faithful.

In answer to that question "What do you feel God is calling you to be and do?" we have been pleased with the number of people who answer that God is calling them to be faithful, to seek ways to live their lives in faithful response to God's love. To be faithful to God is to serve others. Our call is outward, not inward. We are called to use God's gifts—our talents, abilities, and interests—in ways that serve God and others. Serving others is more than being nice to people. It involves justice. It requires our being involved in the pain of the world. Jesus' ministry was to bring good news to the poor, release to the captives, and freedom to the oppressed. And we are called to do the same.

> "My food is to do the will of him who sent me and to complete his work."—Jesus speaks about his call John 4:34

And what does the LORD require of you but to do justice, and to love kindness, and to walk humbly with your God? Micah 6:8

What's exciting is the number of people who are passionate about their vocations and their call from God. It is no accident that there is a relationship between what we are passionate about and God's call to serve. Frederick Buechner says it best: "The place God calls you to is the place where your deep gladness and the world's deep hunger meet."[2] It's quite awesome to consider that God thinks so highly of us as to give us such a huge responsibility.

The Great "Aha!"

The great "Aha!" occurs when it dawns on us that, indeed, we do have a role to play in God's kingdom here on earth; indeed, God is calling me, "little old insignificant me," to do great things as a participant in God's kingdom of love, peace, justice, and grace; indeed, I can make a difference in this world. And should we choose to accept this calling, God will assist us in every way, every day, as we live out our callings.

> "Christian spiritual discernment is the process of listening for God's presence and action in one's life, discriminating between what is of God and what is of some other source."[3]—Sister Elizabeth Liebert

Our jobs as leaders are to point youth and young adults to God, the Creator, and to walk with them on a journey of discovering how to listen for God. On this journey they will hear God calling them to work, to serve, and to live a lifestyle of gratitude and faithfulness. On this journey they can begin to discern the ways in which God's call is played out in their vocations, in their decision making, and in their daily lives.

The Call to Ordained and Nonordained Ministry

In a book on discerning God's call, we would be remiss if we did not speak about the call of God to ordained and nonordained ministry, to those particular occupations of Christian leadership and service. As we said earlier, we all are called to ministry in some form. There are those, however, whom God is calling to serve as pastors, Christian educators, youth ministers, deacons, priests, and missionaries. There are those

whom God is calling to spend two or three years studying Bible, theology, Christian education, and other curricula related to ministry, mission, and service.

The key concepts of this program and the process of listening for God and discovering gifts and skills apply to every call of God, including the call to ordained and nonordained ministry. All these calls require attending the work of the Spirit in hearts and lives. Discerning

God's call to ordained ministry is not a more holy endeavor than discerning any other call. We hear about people who struggle with such a call. But struggle is involved in all calls, as people endeavor to be faithful to what they perceive God is calling them to be and do.

What is distinctive about the call to ordained ministry and other church, mission, and service leadership is the responsibility we in the community of faith have for identifying potential candidates for ministry. The church needs gifted people to lead it into a future marked by diminishing church membership, pervasive secularity, and a lack of values and character formation. The church needs us to help find these people.

We pastors, educators, and lay leaders must pay attention to our role in calling youth and young adults to pastoral and educational ministry. We must speak up when we recognize gifts for ministry. We must ask,

> "The gifts he gave were that some would be apostles, some prophets, some evangelists, some pastors and teachers, to equip the saints for the work of ministry, for building up the body of Christ." Ephesians 4:11–12

"Have you considered ministry? or Christian education?" when we sense a person's passion for God and the church. We must encourage those who have a yearning, a restlessness, or a sense that God may be nudging them in this direction. We must recognize that God calls us to serve as agents of God's call, and therefore we must not remain silent.

A key concept of this career counseling program is that God's call is discovered in community. Community is essential to discerning a call to ordained and nonordained ministry. Responding to such a call involves a commitment to test that call over time through prayerful listening, evaluation of experiences and insights, and practicing faith in community. Persons considering ministry are encouraged—in many denominations, are required—to explore God's call with a group. A discernment group[4] can help a seeker listen for God and work through issues that may not be clear.

How Do We Discover What God Is Calling Us to Be and Do?

This is the core question of career counseling ministry. Youth or young adults and their leaders will spend weeks, maybe months, exploring this question. Although there is no quick and easy answer, the following list of ways to discover God's call can serve as an overview of this exploration:

> Our lifestyle and vocation are our response to God's call.

1. by recognizing that, indeed, God does call us to play a role in God's kingdom here on earth.
2. by learning more about ourselves, the persons God created.
3. by inviting God into the conversation and staying in conversation with God.
4. by practicing the practices of faith (chapter 3).
5. by being in relationship and community with friends, family, significant adult friends, and mentors within the church.
6. by being open to new things, to new understandings about God and how God relates to us.
7. by trying new things, being willing to risk, fail, and then try again.

CHAPTER 3

The Practices of Faith

. . . those who seek me find me.—Proverbs 8:17b (NIV)

A fifty-nine-year-old friend confided that it annoyed her when people talked about God having a plan for our lives. She felt she was living proof that God did not have a plan for her life. She was divorced and recounted a twenty-six-year marriage that should have ended in the first ten years. She never had a job that interested her, and she was tired of the activities that at least gave her something to do. She viewed her life as a waste. She questioned: If God is loving and generous, if God calls people and guides them, then why had God overlooked her?

When, recently, a man whom she cared for "dumped her," as she put it, she was convinced God had abandoned her as well. In our many talks she kept repeating, "I pray, but there's no answer. Just nothing." She had tried church, and even though she enjoyed making new friends, she hadn't gained a sense of God's presence or of God's love for her.

This is not an unusual story. Many people claim Christianity as their religion but don't experience the presence of God. They believe in God but are not sure that God believes in them. They perceive prayer as a one-way communication to God. They go to church but have a hard time "hearing" God.

What's missing? Practice. Listening for God takes practice. Discerning God's will, hearing God's call, requires practice. Practice involves doing something over and over again, until you learn how to do it, or it becomes easier, or it becomes a part of you.

Imagine a basketball team where one player sits out for two months, never coming to a single practice. Then one night he shows up and jumps into the game. He doesn't know the plays. He doesn't know the team members. Everyone's timing is thrown off because of him. Finally, a frustrated player pulls him aside and

says, "You call yourself a basketball player? You don't even know the game."

We may think we know God and know how to "play the game" of faith, but if we don't show up for practice, we really don't know anything about it. Like that basketball player, it's very hard to be a player, a Christian, without practicing faith. Even if we attended church somewhat regularly and prayed when we wanted something from God, we still would have a limited understanding of our Creator. Like the woman described above, our perception of God would be based . . . on what? Surely not on knowledge of God. The God she described is not the God of the Old and New Testaments. Her God is too small. God is much greater than anything we can imagine.

Hearing God's call, being a faithful follower of Jesus Christ, requires the practice of faith. Practices of faith are the things we do to know God better and to live intentionally as followers of Jesus Christ.

> Christian practices mark us as and make us into Jesus' followers. Our salvation comes by grace through faith, not through practice—but Christian practices are means of grace by which God strengthens individuals and the church to live faithfully.[1]
>
> Practices are things that both give us away as Jesus' followers and that shape and mold us into people conformed to God.[2]

The practices of faith are God's way of teaching us how to love God and one another. Without God, there's no such thing as love. It is only because of God's revelation of love for us that we are capable of love. Practices of faith are also God's way of showing us how to play whatever role we are called to play in the revolution of love and grace that is God's intention for the world. It is through the practices of faith that God reveals God's self to us and teaches us how to be faithful. God has provided these disciplines not just for our well-being but as a way of preparing us for service to God and neighbor. If we want to know what God wants us to be and do, we need to know God. To know God, we need to practice faith. The more we practice faith, the better we know God.

Listening for God

If you get real quiet, when you're in bed at night, Jesus will talk to you.—Carlton, age three

Listening for God is a practice of faith. Yet it encompasses all the practices of faith. Listening for God actually is the objective of practicing faith. The practices of faith put us in a position to make space for God, to be aware of God's presence, to "hear" God.

Spirituality is a big issue today. For the last several years, interest in spirituality has blossomed both within the church and beyond. Millions of people are searching for something larger than themselves, hungering for something sacred that can give deeper meaning to life. Many are looking for ways to experience God.

What is ironic about this rebirth is the eagerness of many to avoid the church in their search for the sacred. On the ABC talk show *The View* (March 1999), the four hosts were discussing spirituality and said how pleased they were that the search for God was making a comeback. They were, however, determined to make sure that people didn't feel they have to go to church or belong to an organized religion in order to be spiritual. The conversation seemed to suggest that the church is an archaic institution, to be avoided at all costs. Sadly, that's the impression many people have of "church."

Robert Wuthnow, sociologist of religion, describes a shift in spirituality. Before the 1960s, the spiritual was thought to be located in sacred places, in structural traditions that would naturally be found in the church. Since the 1960s, people have sought the sacred in a variety of places, including other religious traditions, therapy, twelve-step groups, angel sightings, miraculous happenings, and the search for the inner self.[3]

Spirituality today may or may not be associated with God. Many spiritual endeavors tend to substitute psychology for theology. We worry that such efforts only confuse people's understanding of God. We fear a watered-down concept of God that tries to reshape God to fit into popular culture. It makes us shudder to think that someday people might say, "Remember the 1990s, when God and spirituality were popular?" as if God were a trend or fad.

But let's not be too hard on people who are searching for God in some form. They might just run into the one Holy God of Israel, who happens to be searching for them. Studies show that the desire to find purpose and meaning in life is a major concern of today's youth and young adults. This is good news, for meeting that need is exactly what Jesus Christ is all about: "I came that they may have life, and have it abundantly" (John 10:10).

Serving in the area of youth ministry for over twenty-five years has been exciting because, in that time, it's been the young people who have broadened my understanding of the practices of faith. Take, for instance, hands-on mission, which is a practice of faith that transforms youth and youth ministry. By actually doing acts of compassion, youth and young adults come to know Christ and experience God's presence at new levels.

For several years, our church has been taking a large group of senior high students, college students, and adult advisers on a mission to Mexico to build homes for very poor families. Each night we'd gather to reflect on the day's events with a simple ritual or practice, asking, "Where did you see God today?" The first night only a few people spoke, but after several days, the practice taught us how to look for God. It made us keenly aware of God's presence, both during the daily activities of compassion and during the nightly community of sharing and praise.

We in the church continue to fill our calendars with wonderful programs that attract youth and get them involved in the life of the church. But if we neglect to listen for God in these activities, we miss completely the point of what we're doing. For every activity, we should make a habit of asking, "Where is God in this?" "Why do we do this activity?" This awareness of God's presence transforms fellowship activities, studies, service projects, even worship. Our activities will then become practices of faith. The more we practice, the more attuned we become to "hearing" God's call, to perceiving God's will for our lives, individually and collectively.

How Do You Know It's God?

So we pray, and we open our hearts to divine guidance. How do we know that what we hear in response is God? How do we differentiate between our desires and God's will? When is it God's answer to prayer and not our own?

We tackle these questions here, before we begin discussing practices, because it is so easy to get stuck in doubt before you even get started in faith. There is such a thing as healthy doubt, and it means we are struggling with faith issues, not abandoning faith. But doubt can shut us down before we give God a chance. So what should we do? The answer lies in trust. Proverbs 8:17 is reassuring: "those who seek me find me" (NIV). We must trust that God is trying to get through to us, trying to speak. Confessing that we are not good listeners, we ask God to calm our fears, dispel our doubts, and give us direction. Then we ask for the courage to act on what we believe we are hearing from God.

All of this takes practice. Talk with other people about this issue. Talk with those who practice faith. Ask: How do you hear God? How do you know it's God? You'll no doubt hear many of the same answers we have:

> "Now that I am in the habit of being quiet before God during my prayer time, a thought will come to me, and I just know it's from God. It may not be a whole answer to a problem, just a first step, and I feel good about it."
>
> "The way I discern answers or guidance from God is to evaluate whether my action is consistent with what I know about God and Jesus Christ, if it's consistent with scripture, and if it is loving, caring, and serving."
>
> "I'm a fence-sitter. I really believe that it's God when I sense a little voice saying, 'Go for it.'"
>
> "I believe God is talking to me all the time, even when I'm not thinking about God. When I do tune in, the thoughts I get that are good, creative, loving, great ideas, I believe those are from God."

> "Commit your way to the LORD; trust in him, and he will act." Psalm 37:5

The thoughts about how I'm going to nail my competition—they're not from God. Or about how bad I am at this or that, and not worth anything—not from God. When I'm whining, that's probably not from God. I could be whining *to* God. It's okay to whine to God; God just doesn't whine back."

Many people talked about nudges and chills or a little shudder as being their way of recognizing that God was speaking to them. Others said their conscience—their sense of right and wrong—was their way of hearing God. Others cited coincidences as being worthy of sitting up and taking notice—God was trying to get their attention.

Having a "spiritual friend" or a group of people who share in the practices of faith is helpful in discerning God's voice. The career counseling group we describe in this book can provide feedback to group members' experiences of God. A friend can observe something that might have gone unnoticed. A friend can offer insights or ask challenging questions. In this way the group models caring for others. This care for others keeps the group members from being preoccupied with their own issues, their own career worries. Above all, group members recognize that they can hear God's voice through other people.

> Together we are a larger wholeness in Christ than we are alone.[4]

The answer, then, is that we hear God in many ways. But we have to put ourselves in a position to listen. That's why we desperately need to practice faith. Practicing faith becomes a lifestyle. It requires putting God at the center of our lives. To know God, to follow Christ, and to discern God's voice require a commitment of life, mind, and will. Growing in faith and in relationship to Jesus Christ involves a rearrangement of our priorities, a transformation of our values, our lifestyles, and our hearts.

Inviting God into the Conversation

Some people have a hard time with prayer. Perhaps they have encountered the advice to "just pray about it" and found it too simple or off-putting. Others either aren't comfortable with praying or don't know how to talk to God. Because communing with God in some form is what practices of faith are all about, we need to discover a way of talking about prayer and other practices. The phrase "inviting God into the conversation" is helpful in encouraging people to begin to let God in, to let God be a part of their ongoing discussions about life, vocation, and faith.

Each of the career counseling sessions includes a segment titled "Inviting God into the Conversation." This is the time for the group to discuss and implement the practices of faith.

Practices of Faith

What are these practices of faith? In this section we discuss seven practices. We list fifty practices in the career participant's journal (see appendix 1, p. 5 of the journal), and it's not an exhaustive list. In fact, many practices contain practices. For example, within the practice of worship are many practices, such as singing, confession, preaching, and stewardship. The practice of prayer includes many practices or ways to pray. Volumes can be and have been written about faith practices, and we include a few titles in appendix 3. We are not prescribing how a person must experience God. We are not saying everyone has to pray or do daily devotionals in the same way. We are simply inviting everyone to be open to the variety of ways in which God is present.

People of faith tend to categorize ways of expressing and practicing faith as conservative or liberal, fundamental or progressive. Whether we admit it or not, we tend to look for "our" kind of faith expression, "our" kind of worship, and "our" kind of language. Since all God's children are individuals, it's understandable that we are drawn to different styles of worship and faith expression. If our preferences, however, lead us to be judgmental of others' expressions or to seek out only "our" kind of people, we stray from God's intentions for reconciliation and community among God's people.

When I catch myself asking the question "Is it liberal or conservative?" I recall the advice of Sister Ruth, a Benedictine nun whom the writer Kathleen Norris quotes:

> When you come to a place where you have to go left or right, go straight ahead.[5]

Prayer

No doubt the most familiar practice of faith is prayer. Beginning at an early age, we hear and learn prayers—blessings at meals, bedtime prayers, and, of course, the prayer Jesus taught his followers, the Lord's Prayer. We learn to thank God for our blessings, to pray for our family and friends, to ask God to help us with our problems, and to help us be good little girls and boys. We learn many kinds of prayers. We even have aids for learning to pray, such as ACTS, the acronym for adoration, confession, thanksgiving, and supplication. When we gather as the community of faith, we pray—in worship, in Sunday school classes, in fellowship gatherings, on retreats and mission trips.

Not everyone, however, has the same level of comfort about prayer. Many youth and adults feel inadequate when they pray out loud. Many say they're just not good at it. The truth is that God welcomes and hears all prayers. It doesn't matter whether or not we're good at it. In fact, it's natural to feel inadequate before our Creator. The only way to counteract feelings of inadequacy is to pray, to participate in the practice of prayer. The challenge for us educators and leaders is to teach this practice by incorporating prayer into all activities.

Leaders can help career counseling participants become familiar with various ways to pray by incorporating into the sessions several methods of prayer and by sharing ways to pray. Here are a few suggestions:

- Sentence or word prayers (often called popcorn prayer). These can be offered by anyone at any time during a prayer. (No need to "go around the circle" with everyone praying in turn; this can be too much pressure.)
- Silent prayers.
- Breath prayers. In this form of prayer you repeat silently to yourself short phrases, in rhythm with your breathing. For example: while breathing in, say, "Be still," and while breathing out, say, "And know that I am God"; or "Gracious God" (breathe in), "Have mercy on me" (breathe out). Breath prayers help a person eliminate distractions and

> You can't learn to pray
> by reading about prayer;
> you learn to pray by praying.

focus on God. When leading a breath prayer with a group, the leader might say: "Breathe in God's love to you; breathe out God's love to others" or, "Breathe in God's Spirit; breathe out anger or hateful thoughts."

- Responsive prayers. Here the leader prays and the group repeats a response, such as "Hear our prayer, O Lord"; "Great is the Lord and most worthy to be praised!"; "God's love endures forever." The leader tells the group the phrase that will cue them to respond, phrases such as "For this we lift our hearts to you" or "God is faithful." The Psalms are a resource for responsive prayer.
- Conversation prayers. Begin by telling the group that God hears our concerns as we speak them. Start the prayer with a phrase such as "Lord, hear the prayers of your people," then invite people to share their concerns. Close the prayer with another phrase, such as "Thanks be to our good and gracious God, whose love is endless." Eyes do not need to be closed during this prayer, as this form of prayer acknowledges God's presence and invites God into the conversation.
- Pray the Psalms. The Psalm writer speaks both our longings and groanings and our praises and thanksgivings. The Psalms reassure us by affirming and defining who God is.
- Write prayers. A prayer journal can give focus to the practice of prayer. In addition to "praying on paper," the journalers can note particular scripture passages that both speak to them and aid in their praying. They can review what they wrote earlier, recalling specific concerns and joys and noting where God has been present. Reviewing their journal entries helps people to discern how God answers prayers and works in their lives.

Prayer doesn't need to be formal; it doesn't need a beginning, a middle, and an end. Encourage people to understand prayer as talking to God, so that youth and young adults can get into the habit of praying at all times of the day, in all circumstances, as 1 Thessalonians 5:17 advises us to do. In the career counseling sessions (chapters 8 through 13), we speak of prayer as inviting God into the conversation. This concept suggests overlaying our "daily life" with our "faith life." To use computer language, it's like templating our daily concerns and decision making with God's presence. God is aware of all that goes on in our lives. With the practice of prayer, we invite God into our conversations with family, with friends, and with ourselves, as we talk about our struggles, worries, decisions, and joys. As prayer becomes more a part of our lives, we find talking to ourselves and to God can become one and the same.

Prayer is not a monologue addressed to God. A relationship implies two-way communication. And yet listening for God is the hard part. We are not good at being silent and giving God a chance to speak to us. But it is the listening for God that enables us to grow in faith.

Prayer can actually be thought of as incorporating two practices. The first is setting aside time for prayer. To get to know God, we need to set aside a piece of our day for God. It's hard. We're busy. We have great intentions. We fail. But we keep trying. If we want God to shape us into being players in the divine plan for the world, then we have to take up this practice of faith. This is where the term *discipline of faith* hits home, for it takes discipline to set aside time just to be with God.

Many people start the day with prayer and meditation. That's hard for those of us who are not morning people. I spent years feeling guilty that I didn't get up a little earlier to pray—but morning isn't the only time we can pray, or even the best. Lunchtime, late afternoon, bedtime are all appropriate times. People need to experiment to find what's best for them. Theologically, any time is good. It's good to dedicate the day to the Lord. It's also good to pause in the middle of the day, letting God bring peace and insight. Praying in the evening and looking back on the day, which in the Roman Catholic tradition is called the *examen*, gives opportunity for reflecting, for seeing where God was present, and for identifying the blocks that prevented recognition of God's presence.

How do you begin praying? Start with ten minutes, and work toward twenty or thirty minutes. People find that once time set aside for God becomes a practice, a habit, they want more. In the struggle to find the time, many write "God" in their appointment books.

The second practice of prayer is having a continuing, regular conversation with God that is at the heart of a "lifestyle of prayer." This involves developing a "consciousness of God" at all times, an awareness in which we find ourselves, throughout the day, expressing to God words of gratitude, petition, frustration, anger, forgiveness, love, adoration, confession, awe. We sense God's awareness of all that goes on in our lives. We sense God's blessing and guidance. It's a way of life that invites God into the conversation of our "stuff," our joys and concerns, our cares and griefs.

Meditation

The idea of meditating may conjure up images of Eastern religions or the New Age movement. In reality, meditation is as old as prayer. It is reflecting on a passage or theme with the intention of deepening one's understanding and insight. In ancient Israel, the Jews were instructed to meditate on the law day and night (Joshua 1:8).

Meditation requires time set aside. Meditating involves reading a short passage and thinking, feeling, and praying its words. The passage should be short so that you can have time to actually meditate on the words. Longer readings tend to pull one's focus away from meditation. Don't confuse meditation with reading and studying, however, for they are very different. In meditation, a particular word or phrase will bring forward an image or thought that will then serve as an opening through which the Spirit leads us into deeper meaning. At that point we stop reading and make space for God to speak to us.

Much that we have learned about meditation comes from *lectio divina*, or holy reading, an exercise that is part of the Benedictine monastic tradition. *Lectio divina* has four parts:

1. Slow, meditative reading of a brief passage
2. Reflection on the passage
3. Prayer to God
4. Contemplative prayer (listening for God)

The scriptures are the natural place to start the practice of meditation. Devotional books are another resource. It is easy to be distracted, to think about things you have to do, especially when beginning this practice. If you become distracted, jot down what you need to remember and continue meditating. As people become better at meditating, they find they don't worry about distractions.

Don't expect to master this practice immediately. If the time you spend meditating doesn't seem to have any results, don't give up. Try doing it a different way. If we are truly open to the possibility of God working in our lives, God will transform us. Prayer transforms us. We can trust that in the process of praying, God teaches us to pray. In the process of meditating, God teaches us to meditate.

Meditation brings us into a greater awareness of the relevance of God's word to our everyday lives. The following are some hints to help you develop the practice of meditation:

- Read the passage several times, at least once aloud. Read slowly. Be aware of any particular word or phrase that seems to jump out at you. Perhaps memorize a verse or phrase that speaks to you.
- If you are reading a story—a biblical passage, for example—put yourself in the scene as one of the characters.

- Think about ways the passage relates to your life. Reflect on this.
- Answer the questions listed under "Journal Writing" in the next section.
- Keep a journal of your reflections and prayers.
- Spend at least as much time in contemplative prayer as you do in prayer to God.
- Pay careful attention in particular to what God may be saying to you.
- Focus on your breathing.
- Experiment with different times, places, and ways to meditate.

Journal Writing

Journal writing is a companion practice to meditation. It is helpful for clarifying thoughts and decisions. Looking back on our writings gives us a chance to see where we have been in our journey of discovery about God and ourselves. As thoughts come to mind, write them down. Write prayers. Write scripture or quotes from other resources. Begin each day by listing three things for which you are grateful. Write thoughts you have about an action or decision you are contemplating. Answer some of the questions listed here:

Where did you see God today?
Where do you see God at work in your life—at work, at school, at home, in relationships, in recreation, in sabbath time?
What do you feel God is saying to you at this time?
Is there something you need to do? or to refrain from doing? Why?
Is God calling you to act or to wait?
What is preventing you from acting?
What are you grateful for?

Reading our prayers of anguish or reviewing the pros and cons of a decision we've made sheds light on how God is working in our lives. Often we find ourselves praying a prayer written months before. Remember to date entries.

Leaders in the career counseling sessions should encourage journal writing. A set of journal pages is included in appendix 1 and can also be downloaded from the Presbyterian Publishing Corp. Web site, www.ppcpub.com, for use on computers. Journals are personal. Individuals are invited to share from their journals, but only if they so desire. Some people are more receptive to keeping a journal than others. We encourage everyone to give it a try.

Worship

Worship is the central practice of the Christian community. Worship is time set aside in community and in communion with fellow believers, time given to praising and thanking our generous, loving Creator. In *The Godbearing Life: The Art of Soul Tending for Youth Ministry*, Kenda Dean and Ron Foster call worship an "immersion experience" in the Christian way of life.[6] As I write this, the season of Pentecost has begun. Yesterday, Pentecost Sunday, our morning worship service was exactly that—an immersion experience in the Christian way of life. We had a baptism, the confirmation of young people who were publicly affirming their faith, ordination of officers, communion, and a sermon that challenged us to live faithfully and serve. The music tied the service together. One member of the church remarked: "Anyone wanting to know what the Christian faith is all about should have been here today."

In worship, we have opportunities to practice many of our practices of faith. Yesterday, for example, we practiced prayer (praise, confession, thanksgiving, intercession, petition, blessing), hymn singing, affirmation of faith, baptism, the Lord's Supper, confirmation, ordination, stewardship, and preaching. In and around our worship together, we practiced gratitude, hospitality, forgiveness, compassion, ministry, service, and study. When we recognize the number of practices that we can do on one Sunday morning, we can see why worship is at the center of the Christian faith.

For many leaders of youth, worship is a challenge. Many of us underestimate our young people and buy into the notion that worship is off-putting to youth and young adults. So we focus on other activities, leaving impressionable adolescents to grow into adulthood with little notion of what it's like to experience God through the practice of regular worship. This does them a great disservice. Kenda Dean and Ron Foster further affirm the centrality of worship, especially for adolescents:

> The irony is that, developmentally, adolescents *need* a transcendent God worthy of their fidelity, a God who can transport them beyond the limitations of self. Millennial youth have cut their teeth on special effects and simulations of transcendence and are in search of the life-shaking, real article. Domesticating these practices succeeds only in dimming their wattage at a time when adolescents seek high-voltage . . . encounters with the sacred.
>
> Rather than "taming" practices of worship that bring us into God's presence, implying

that youth cannot handle direct sacred experience, we are called to create welcoming, undiluted worship that embraces the creative contributions and honors the critiques of adolescents who know real transcendence when they see it.[7]

Sabbath Keeping

"Remember the sabbath day, and keep it holy" is the familiar fourth commandment, found in Exodus 20:8. Two practices are implied in this commandment. The first is worship—devoting the sabbath to the Lord your God (v. 10). The second is rest, as when the Lord rested on the seventh day after six days of creating heaven, earth, the sea, and all that is in them (v. 11). We Christians may do a fair job of worshiping God on the sabbath. But we are not good at resting. Even nonworkaholics face enough assignments and pressures in work and life that they feel as if they never have time to breathe. And breathing is exactly what God is calling us to do—to rest and allow the Spirit to breathe in and through us. Besides, in a world of competition for control and power, we need a day when we let go and let God run the world for the day. Keeping sabbath reminds us that the earth, time, and our lives belong to the Lord.

Rest is essential to the abundant life about which Christ speaks. It's difficult to grow in knowledge of God, to sustain a relationship with our Lord, and thus to know God's will, if our lives are filled with busyness. We must practice sabbath rest. Part of our rest can be spent in prayer or meditation, but part of it needs to be spent in a cessation of activity. In times of rest, we make space for God; we listen for God and give God a chance to reach us. Patricia Loring, writer on Quaker spirituality, emphasizes that sabbath time is more than just Sunday worship:

> It's truly time-out for God: an X drawn through the appointment book, phone off the hook, time for rest, for recreation, for quiet presence to what is, time for the unexpected to arise, for meditative reflection, for encounter with the divine outside the hour formally scheduled. . . .
>
> Life that does not include this temple built of time . . . this contemplative space, leaves no opening to sense the divine rhythm, the holy dance of life, the invitation to our particular figure in the dance; no quiet to hear the still, small voice; no room to be drawn into the fullness of Life God offers us.[8]

Many of us in church professions find that Sunday is not a day of rest, and so we must practice sabbath on another day. Some recommend taking an hour a day, a day a week, a week a year for sabbath time. Explore with youth and young adults what sabbath might look like for them. Play with ideas. How about a sabbath retreat? Appendix 2 contains an example of a spirituality retreat that can be used for youth or young adults. It is simply time set aside to practice some of these practices, including prayer, meditation, reflection, and silence.

Presence

Have you ever gone to visit someone after the death of their loved one and felt awkward because you didn't know what to say? Have you ever avoided the situation for that very reason? I'll never forget the relief I felt the first time someone explained, "It doesn't matter what you said; it matters that you were there." It became clear to me that God was speaking through that person, for that one memorable statement changed my attitude and my willingness to enter into another's grief and pain. It is even clearer now that "being there" is a practice of faith.

God's gift to us is God's presence. The practices of faith teach us to recognize God's presence. When we get that job, celebrate the birth of a child, arrive somewhere safely, resolve a conflict, or receive an unexpected blessing, God is present with us. When we lose a job or girlfriend or loved one, or when we are devastated, depressed, broken, or alone, God is present with us. God models presence. In like manner, we are called to be present with one another.

Adult leaders teach the practice of being present by modeling presence. Many young people and young adults are already adept at this practice and don't realize it. Many have sat with (been present with) friends through breakups of relationships, roommate problems, and various other disappointments, yet not recognized that they are in ministry. They are practicing presence, the ministry of being there. We need to affirm youth and young adults in their ministry of presence by talking about these experiences and naming these acts of presence as a practice of faith.

There's a familiar story about a mother who asked her six-year-old why she stayed so long at her friend's house. She explained that her friend's doll had broken. Her mom asked if she had helped her friend fix it. "No," she replied, "I helped her cry."

Embodying

In her book *Listening Spirituality*, Quaker teacher and writer Patricia Loring adds a fifth stage, embodying, to the meditation exercise, the *lectio divina*—which consists of, for her, reading, reflection, active prayer, contemplative prayer, and embodying. She defines embodying as "fulfilling and living out the nudges of the Spirit."[9] It is the active response to what is discerned during a time of meditation. Embodying is the doing of what we perceive God calling us to do at that time or during that day. "At a more profound level, it is the life of the transformed person, living out of a will increasingly yielded to and united with God's will."[10]

Embodying means living our faith. It is living a lifestyle of faithfulness, gratitude, grace, service, justice, mission, ministry, and compassion. And remember that all of these lifestyles are practices. They are ways in which we practice faith. And they all involve transformation. Without God, we cannot do any of them. Resentment, hatred, prejudice, self-absorption, greed, power lust, and fear have an insidious way of controlling our minds and hearts. When we open ourselves to the transforming power and love of our Creator, our attitudes and instincts are transformed. We find that our reactions change: we have compassion instead of criticism, gratitude instead of resentment. We find, often quite to our surprise, that paralyzing fear can be overcome, allowing us to respond to the Lord's command in Micah:

> What does the LORD require of you but to do justice, and to love kindness, and to walk humbly with your God? Micah 6:8

A Challenge

We have talked about only seven practices of faith—prayer, meditation, journal writing, worship, sabbath keeping, presence, and embodying—and have mentioned several others under worship and embodying. There are many more, including Bible study, instruction, tithing, sharing faith, hospitality, healing, solitude, fasting, prayer walking, spiritual direction, simplicity, and creating memories (which we discuss in chapter 5). An extensive list of practices is found on pages 5 and 6 of the journal (see appendix 1). We challenge you and your youth or young adults to try practices that are new to you. Go on a spiritual retreat. Check out ecumenical retreat programs, such as Walk to Emmaus and Cursillo. Even if it is not exactly "you"—not something you could see yourself doing—do it anyway. Try it. Stretch yourself.

There is no shortcut to discerning God's will. There is no quick and easy formula to discovering what God is calling us to be and do. The answer lies in getting to know God better. And that's why we've included a whole chapter on practices.

Practices bring us closer to God and God's intentions for us. They increase our trust in the Lord. They enable the Holy Spirit to move within and through us. With practice, walking with God gradually takes less effort and fewer reminders. It becomes almost second nature.

One of the best gifts adult leaders can give youth and young adults is to introduce them to the practices of faith. It is one thing to teach about the importance of a relationship with God. It is quite another thing to offer tools to experience that relationship. Invite youth and young adults to come with you and to listen for what God is doing.

Our youth and young adults can learn how to hear God's voice in the midst of confusing and competing voices. They can experience a transformation of life and lifestyle in which, as Loring notes, the Spirit enables an "openness to being prepared for we-never-know-what. The great thing is dancing to a rhythm of life that is not established by one's self. . . . It's established by 'The Lord of Life,' 'The Lord of the Dance'. . . . Our practice and devotion is to help us be attuned to hear, flexible enough to respond to, the unexpected shifts, syncopations and moods of the rhythm of the dance."[11]

When youth and young adults become more familiar with practices, they have a better sense of self, of God, and of who they are in relationship with God. They have skills for living a life of faith and gratitude. They are more confident about facing the dilemmas of the "what next." They seem to have a head start on their peers at this critical time in life, when there are so many decisions to make. Thus, because of their faith experience, they can help their peers who are struggling with the same dilemmas.

Trust in the LORD, and do good;
  so you will live in the land, and enjoy security.
Take delight in the LORD,
  and he will give you the desires of your heart.
Commit your way to the LORD;
  trust in him, and he will act. . . .
Be still before the LORD, and wait patiently for him.
                                        Psalm 37:3–5, 7

CHAPTER 4

A Design for Career Counseling Ministry with Youth and Young Adults

See, I am doing a new thing! . . . I am making a way in the desert.—Isaiah 43:19 (NIV)

This verse from Isaiah is a source of comfort, hope, and challenge. It is a source of comfort because many youth and young adults are experiencing desert times in their search for a meaningful life. It is a source of hope that God is doing a new thing in their lives. And it is a challenge to stay with God and see that new thing take shape.

One of the new things that God is doing in our churches is calling us to do career counseling ministry with youth and young adults. The target groups for this ministry—high school juniors and seniors and young adults—are traditionally the hardest to keep involved in the church. Though they are not necessarily losing faith or abandoning God, young people and young adults, even those who have been active, drop out of sight because there's too much going on in their lives. As they struggle with decisions, unknowns, and pressures, church falls to a lower priority. How ironic! The church may be just what they need—a place where they can be nurtured and find support as they wrestle with life issues. The challenge for the church is to reach out to youth and young adults and say, "We want to walk with you on a journey of discovering who you are and what God is calling you to be and do in your lifestyle and vocation."

The career counseling program is a ministry designed to provide a small-group setting where youth or young adults can be comfortable talking about themselves, God, work, faith, and lifestyle with caring leaders from the congregation. The program can be as short as six weeks of ninety-minute sessions, one session per week, or it can develop into a long-term ministry, in which career groups meet frequently and mentor relationships flourish.

The program is designed for young adults and for juniors and seniors in high school. Even though vocational thinking and planning should begin at an even younger age, this particular program works best with juniors and seniors, for they are feeling the decision-making time crunch as graduation draws closer.

The term *young adults* covers a broad range of individuals and circumstances. The program we write of here ministers to post–high school young adults—those who are in college, those who are working, and those who are looking for their first job. It also attracts young adults in their twenties and early thirties who aren't sure about issues of career, lifestyle, and God's call. Even those youth and young adults who know what they want to do or who are already doing it enjoy having the opportunity to deepen their faith and make connections between vocation and a meaningful life.

The Career Counseling Group

The career counseling ministry program is a small-group ministry, rather than one-on-one counseling. Each group should have two to five participants and one or two leaders. The ratio should be at least one leader for every three or four participants. Thus, if there were six participants, you would form two groups.

The sessions are specifically designed to be appropriate for both youth and young adults. We believe that youth are capable of exploring the same questions about faith and life as young adults. The answers and discussions will vary, depending on the ages involved, but the issues are valid for both. As we mentioned, if you are having career ministry for youth, the groups will be composed of juniors and seniors. If the focus is young adults, groups can be composed of all ages. If there are a large number of young adults interested in the program, then form groups of similar ages.

At the first session, participants and leaders decide when and how frequently they will meet; usually groups meet weekly.

Being part of the group is vital to the journey of self-discovery and discernment of God's call. A journey is richer when we have fellow sojourners. Group members encourage one another and learn from each others' insights and experiences. They learn more about God, as other people's viewpoints help clarify their own understanding of God. They learn more about themselves when they have feedback from others. Insights, perspectives, and experiences shared can bring all group members closer to God and to one another.

Leadership of the Group

One or two leaders are needed for each career counseling group. Look for people who will be willing to walk with several youth or young adults on a journey of discovering what God is calling them to be and do. These leaders will become significant adult friends to the participants. Look for people who see life as a response in faith to God and who are active in the life of the church.

Consider those who have served or are serving as leaders in youth or young adult ministry, for they would already be familiar with the age group. Look for people who are good listeners and are willing to learn and grow along with the participants. It is best that leaders not be the parents or guardians of a participant, for this is a time for developing significant adult friends in the church, other than (or in addition to) parents, who can guide and assist in this journey of discovery.

In the "Introduction to the Sessions" (page 63), we provide guidelines for leaders. Each session contains a section titled "Thinking It Through" that offers background information and suggestions for leading the session.

Nine Key Concepts of Career Counseling Ministry

This career counseling program is based on nine key concepts that serve as a theological foundation for this ministry. What follows is an overview of each concept. Leaders must read chapter 2 on God's call to better understand the concepts. Leaders will also need to read chapter 3 on the practices of faith.

1. You Are Created in God's Image. You Are a Person of Infinite Worth.

Too many people have negative self-images. When we begin to view ourselves as created in the image of God, as reflecting God's love and goodness, and as being people of infinite worth, our self-esteem should soar. God chooses to see us not as the sinful people we are but as God's beloved children, redeemed and restored through Jesus Christ. When we believe the truth about God's relationship to us, we are less likely to turn away from God out of fear that God is displeased with us. God loves us beyond anything we can imagine.

Throughout the career sessions, the participants are encouraged to discover their God-given gifts and to recognize the ways in which God affirms them.

2. God Is Your Partner in Exploring, Discovering, and Living Life.

Once we recognize that God has created us in God's own image and has this incredible love for us, it is possible to see how God desires to partner with us in this venture called life. The participants are encouraged to affirm God as partner and to be open to God as they explore the issues of the kind of vocation to pursue and the kind of life to lead.

3. You Are Co-Creator with God. God Created the World and Invites You to Continue That Creative Work to Help Make the World What God Intended It to Be.

This is another esteem-building concept. The idea of being a co-creator with God could strike some people as blasphemous, as if we were trying to assume equal status with God. On the contrary, we should be humbled by the notion that God regards us as capable of playing a significant role in God's creation. And that is what we are called to do—to continue God's creative work of making the world what God intended it to be.

The Bible confirms our call to be a blessing to others, to serve God and neighbor. The participants will explore their role in God's creation.

4. The Key Is to Stay in Conversation with God.

To discover what God is calling us to be and do, we need to stay in conversation with God. There are many ways to engage in such a dialogue. Participants will look at several practices of faith and will practice them as part of the program. Practices are the ways in which we listen for God and live or "practice" our faith.

5. You Can't Make a Mistake.

This concept gets people's attention. Who ever heard of not making mistakes? Don't we learn from mistakes? Of course we do, and that's why we aren't calling them mistakes. They are learning experiences. This is helpful for participants who are scared of making the wrong career decision, for this concept can give them the confidence to move forward and make decisions.

6. The Question Is Not "What Do You Want to Do When You Grow Up?" Rather, the Question Is "What Do You Want to Do *First*?"

A large percentage of people today are not in the same vocation they chose when they graduated from high school. You may have to point this out to participants at first, but once you do, this is probably the most freeing idea participants come across. Many feel that on graduation from high school or college, they must decide what they want to do for the rest of their lives.

That is too overwhelming a task. Asking, "What do you want to do first?" makes the dilemma manageable. In our modern world of multiple careers and jobs, figuring out what you want to do first makes sense.

7. Career Is Not Just about Doing; It's Also about Being: Ask, "What Is God Calling You to *Be* and *Do*?"

In a world where worth is measured by what we do, it's important to look at who we are, and whose we are. Being God's children gives us incredible worth. Participants will look at who they are as God's own and what that means in the grand scheme of things.

8. God Calls You to a Lifestyle, Not Just a Career or Occupation.

It's important to look at the whole of life, not just our work. God calls us to more than just career. Participants will explore values and lifestyle issues to discover the kind of life God is calling them to live.

9. God's Call Is Discovered in Community (the We-ness of the Call).

Relationships are important. That's why small groups are fundamental to this ministry. We do not discover God's call alone. We need the confirmation of those who know and care about us that we indeed are hearing God's call. Participants will have the support of a group as they explore issues of career, lifestyle, and faith. Friends, family, mentors, teachers, and significant adult friends in the church play vital roles in this process.

The Career Counseling Ministry Program

The basic design consists of six ninety-minute sessions. It is essential that the material in these six sessions be covered. In addition, to get the most from the program, we recommend additional sessions, the development of a mentor relationship between the participant and a church member, and regular journaling. We also recommend using the parent session and parent-participant session described in chapter 5. Leaders of this program should read chapters 2 through 6. For information on youth or young adults with special needs, leaders should read chapter 7.

The Six Sessions

The program is divided into six sessions and covers three topics: "God's Calling," "About You," and "The World of Work." The boundaries of each discussion are flexible, however, and the topics are not exclusive to a particular session. For example, the participants will be discussing God's call throughout the six sessions, even though "God's Calling" is the topic of sessions 1 and 2.

Session 1—"God's Calling: Your Life." In this session, participants look back at their past and forward to their futures in an exercise called "My Life Line." By highlighting major events and activities, they will be able to identify their values, things that are important to them, and identify where God has been present. Participants will begin exploring God's call and the ways in which people "hear" God calling them. Group members are encouraged to share the life-line activity with parents, stepparents, grandparents, and guardians and to consider how parents and guardians can be partners in the career exploration process. The journal and practices of faith are introduced in this session.

Session 2—"God's Calling: Your Dream." This session includes a guided fantasy exercise in which participants envision a day in their lives ten years in the future. They will look at the creation story and consider the roles God calls people to play in God's world. Informational interviews and mentors are introduced in this session.

Session 3—"About You: Skills, Gifts, and Interests." This is the first of two sessions that help participants learn about themselves. Good career counseling helps people know themselves, so they can make better decisions about vocation. In the "Skills and Experiences" exercise, participants identify the skills they use in various activities. "Discovering Your Gifts" is a list of attributes that, when seen as gifts from God, help individuals perceive themselves as persons of worth. At this session, group members identify their interests and begin looking at their assets, those traits or characteristics people have "going for them," resources for facing the future.

In this session, participants share the results of the Myers-Briggs Type Indicator (MBTI), provided they have taken the MBTI. We encourage participants to take the MBTI, a popular indicator of how a person functions, based on his or her preferences. Many in your groups may already have taken it. Others can check schools, colleges, and counseling centers to find counselors who are certified to administer the test. There is cost involved, since trained counselors interpret the test results and give clients a personal assessment. The MBTI is available online from Paladin Associates, Inc. (www.paladinexec.com).

The Keirsey Temperament Sorter II is a shorter version of the MBTI and uses the same sixteen four-letter personality types (e.g., INFP, ESTJ). You can find this test online at www.keirsey.com and in *Please Understand Me II: Temperament, Character, Intelligence* by David Keirsey.[1]

Session 4—"About You: Values, Lifestyle, and Risk." This session continues the process of self-discovery by looking at the issues of values and lifestyle and risk taking. In addition, group members will examine the ways in which a family can be an asset and a challenge in decision making regarding vocation and lifestyle.

Session 5—"The World of Work: Career Fields." In this session, participants are invited to make connections between the information they have learned about themselves and the possibilities in the world of work. Using Holland's clusters of occupations, group members will discuss career fields and perhaps begin to better identify or narrow their choices. John Holland, researcher and professor emeritus at Johns Hopkins University, discovered that people's preferences for work environments and job interests can be clustered into one or more of six categories: Realistic, Investigative, Artistic, Social, Enterprising, and Conventional.

Session 6—"The World of Work: Making Plans." In this session, the group continues the exploration of vocations with a discussion of job site visits. Participants are to arrange visits with people who hold jobs in careers in which they have interest. Group members who already have jobs are encouraged to visit job sites as well. Work habits and life skills are also discussed. The session closes with a blessing on each participant.

The Structure of Each Session

Each session is designed to be approximately ninety minutes. Length depends, of course, on the number of participants. For that reason, we do not indicate the amount of time each activity should take. Each session begins with background information for the leader. As we have already stressed, leaders must read chapters 2 and 3 as preparation for leading the sessions. Leaders must also read chapter 5 in order to lead the parent session and the parent-participant session.

Overview, Thinking It Through, and Preparation

Each session begins with an overview, which highlights the content of the session. This is followed by a time for "thinking it through," which contains helps for leaders such as suggestions for leading an exercise and comments on what to expect from a discussion. The preparation section lists resources for each session. In chapters 2 and 3, you will find help for introducing God's call and the practices of faith.

Inviting God into the Conversation

Each session begins and ends with some form of prayer. We speak of prayer as "inviting God into the conversation," and we hope by this to engage those who may think of God as being remote and unconnected to daily life. The idea of inviting God into conversations appeals to people who would never think of praying in situations such as career decision times, when they are in the midst of intense discussions about what to do with their lives. What happens when they *do* invite God in? Some say it makes them feel more natural, more at ease, praying. Some say it helps them sense God's involvement in their everyday lives.

In response to the question "What is God calling you to be and do?" one twenty-two-year-old college graduate said: "God's call—that's something I'm struggling with. I believe God is calling me *to* Him, but we have things to settle between us. It's a process; it's gradual." I smiled as she explained all this, for she was giving a lovely description of what it means to be in conversation with God.

The most common concern of career participants is that they are not doing or won't know what God wants them to do. They are not sure they are hearing God correctly. The college graduate expressed it well when she said it is a process, and it is gradual. Participants need to be reassured that God wants to reach them. God wants them to hear and understand God's call. What is most reassuring is that God will not give up on them.

> "Let each of you lead the life . . . to which God called you."
> 1 Corinthians 7:17

The Question of the Day

In each session, the question of the day serves as an icebreaker, a conversation starter, a way for each group member to have a turn speaking, and a good way for participants to learn about one another. A list of these questions is on page 3 of the journal. (See appendix 1).

Insight from Scripture

For people to learn about God and God's relationship to us, they need to read and use the Bible. Each session includes a short Bible study on passages that are related to topics discussed in the sessions:

Session 1: Ecclesiastes 3:1–8. Topic: time
Session 2: Genesis 1. Topic: the creation story
            Genesis 12:2. Topic: blessed to be a blessing
Session 3: 1 Corinthians 12. Topic: diversity of gifts
Session 4: Book of Ruth. Topic: family, risks, and loyalty

Session 5: 1 Samuel 3:1–8. Topic: calling and mentors
Session 6: Matthew 14:22–33. Topic: fear and risk

(See chapter 14, which lists additional passages that can be used.)

We recommend that each group member have a Bible and use it during the sessions. Everyone needs practice using the Bible. Handing out copies of a scripture passage robs participants of the opportunity to become more familiar with their Bibles.

The instructions for the Bible study suggest that a leader read the passage while participants follow along. Reading requires preparation, and if it becomes the group practice that members read passages, ask for a volunteer in advance, so they can prepare.

Activity Sheets

In each session, participants will use activity sheets designed to help them discover gifts, skills, and interests. They will become accustomed to reflecting, after each exercise, on the question "What did you discover or learn about yourself?" Activity sheets are found at the end of each session in which they are used. In field testing, both youth and young adults have responded positively to these exercises. Even those who knew what career they wanted to pursue or who were already in that vocation found the activity sheets helpful. If your group is able to visit a career center, these sheets will be valuable to the counselors. Permission to copy the sheets is granted with the purchase of this book.

Practices of Faith

The most perplexing question for participants is "How do you know? How do you discover what God is calling you to be and do?" It is difficult to hear God if we don't practice listening. Practices of faith are the things we do as Christians to listen for God and to act out our faith. Practices may be new to group members. In each session, participants will have opportunities to discuss and share experiences as they try some of the practices. (For a discussion of practices, see chapter 3.)

The Journal

One of the most valuable features of this career counseling ministry is journal writing. The journal is found in appendix 1 and can be copied as needed. Those who would like to keep their journals on their computers can log on to the Presbyterian Publishing Corp. Web site (www.ppcpub.com) and click on Download Materials. Unless participants bring laptops to the sessions, each person will need a printed copy.

The journals are used in every session, so participants should bring them every week. Group members usually see the value in journaling and often continue writing in their journals after the sessions end, and in a number of cases for years. Advise participants to date their entries, so they can look back and see how their values, concerns, interests, and perspectives change over time.

Not everyone takes to journal writing, but we recommend that you encourage the use of the journal during the career counseling course. It can serve as an aid for reflection. For introverts, having time to reflect is essential, as they may not be able to share what they feel or think during the sessions. Extroverts benefit from reflection as well, though they may need encouragement to reflect.

Assignments

Each session ends with an assignment—sharing the life-line activity with parents or guardians; journal writing; filling out an activity sheet; looking for mentors and people to interview; trying practices of faith; visiting job sites. None of the assignments is lengthy. All are activities that encourage personal growth in faith, lifestyle, and career exploration.

Since assignments are usually not a popular feature of any class, leaders need to discuss the importance of these short assignments and seek group members' suggestions for ways to get the assignments done. Encourage the participants' ownership of the career counseling ministry. They are the ones to make it work. They need to decide how to get the most out of the program.

Informational Interviews

At the end of session 2, you will find an "Informational Interview Form" that lists questions for participants to ask people about their careers. Over the course of the program, each participant should contact three or four people who have jobs that interest that participant or who are people the participant admires. He or she will interview these people, recording their answers on the form. This activity encourages participants to get out and look at real careers and jobs. It involves contacting people, a skill necessary for networking, which is a key method for seeking employment.

Job Site Visits

In session 6, you will find a description of job site visits. As they did with informational interviews, participants will contact people who have vocations in which they are interested. This time they will ask to visit the workplace and talk with employees on site. Individuals who visit a potential career-choice job site receive valuable information that will inform their choices. Too many people prepare for careers without ever spending time at a work site. Being part of a group is helpful in exploring job sites, as group members can suggest contacts.

Mentors

Mentors are a valuable asset in the development of a person's calling and vocation. If your church already has a mentor program, find out how it might fit with the career counseling program. If you don't have such a program, consider finding mentors for the career participants; guidelines appear in chapter 6. Group members are encouraged to look for potential mentors and to recognize people who mentor them, even those who aren't long-term, designated mentors.

Parents and Guardians

Parents, stepparents, grandparents, and guardians can be an incredible asset on the career journey. Besides having experience, they have a vested interest in the success of the son, daughter, or family member who is going through the program. In chapter 5, we discuss the roles parents can play, and we include (1) a session for parents and guardians, which would take place before the participants' sessions begin, and (2) a session for parents/guardians and participants, which could be held at any time during the process.

We originally developed the parent/guardian sessions to be used with parents of youth. We found, however, that they give young adults an opportunity to relate to their parents or guardians on a new level, as partners on the career journey. Parents sometimes need to get out of the "parent" role. Likewise, young adults sometimes need to get beyond their fear of being failures in the eyes of their parents. In this program, parents/guardians and their young adult children can become partners in the exploration of faith, values, interests, and vocation. The concept of parents as partners works well with both youth and young adults.

Every effort should be made to involve parents or guardians in this process. Parents need to understand this ministry and the key concepts behind it. They need assurance that the program is worth the effort. They also need to explore their role as partners. (See chapter 5 for information on parents as partners.)

Additional Sessions

We strongly recommended continuing this program beyond the six sessions. Once a group has begun successfully sharing vocational and faith questions, it should be given the opportunity to continue. We leave the number and frequency of these additional sessions to the discretion of your group. Additional sessions will, for one thing, offer time for more informational interviews and job site visits. Participants will enjoy "checking in" with one another on job search, college search, mentor updates, journaling, practices of faith, and decision making.

Career Counseling Center Visit

We recommend that your group schedule a one- or two-day visit to an interdenominational career center. These centers offer testing instruments and inventories in the areas of interests, skills, values, learning styles, personality types, and emotional intelligence. Counselors help clients relate test results to career plans. They offer a variety of resources—print, software, Internet—on occupations, education, military opportunities, and job training.

The advantage of interdenominational career centers is that group members receive individual interpretation of tests by trained counselors. Each client receives an extensive report two or three weeks after the visit. Because they are faith based, these career centers take values and faith issues seriously and complement the career counseling program offered in this book. Since these centers are a ministry and are nonprofit, their services are likely to be less expensive than secular programs.

There are not many such centers in the country, however, so unless you are up for a road trip (and why not?), center visits may not be feasible. See appendix 3 for a list of interdenominational career centers. If a center visit is not feasible, check high schools, colleges, or counseling services to see which testing instruments are offered. As we mentioned in chapter 1, always check out the type of counseling offered, as well as the cost of services. Also check the Internet.

College Trips

Career counseling ministry to young people and church-sponsored college trips can go hand in hand. Youth love road trips, and we've found college trips to be very popular. Each year we ask our juniors and seniors to list their top four choices of colleges. Then we decide which three (sometimes four) schools can be visited on a two- or three-night trip. Trips often require missing a day of school. Many schools allow an excused absence for college visits.

Because our visits are usually on weekends, many admissions offices are closed, and the full services they offer are not available. This is not usually a problem, as we prefer getting tour guides from campus ministries and local church contacts. In this way our young people meet collegiates who manage to stay active in churches and ministries during their college years, and our youth come to realize they can do the same. We do meet with admissions counselors whenever possible. We also try to arrange classroom visits.

When we ask our young people to list colleges they'd like to visit, we also ask them to suggest possible dates for the trip. For our youth, weekends are best. You may find that your juniors and seniors prefer taking three days of a vacation week for the trip. Summer also may be a possibility. Even though activity slows down on many campuses during the summer, you can still have contact with students and admissions counselors. Call the admissions office and ask about the availability of students and recommendations for dates to visit.

Admissions counselors applaud our efforts. They tell us that, since most campus visits are made with families, it's the parents who usually ask the questions. They note that our young people are more willing to ask questions and engage in conversation than the average student visitor. We spend our travel time in lively discussion of the schools. Those who have participated in a career counseling group seem to benefit most from these discussions, as they are accustomed to exploring lifestyle issues, career preparation, and faith. They have a better sense of what to look for on a campus visit.

Parents appreciate our college trips, as we often eliminate the need for them to visit certain schools. Our trips help youth narrow their college choices. And if a young person is interested in a school, she can make a return visit with her family. Many schools invite students to return for an overnight visit.

Guidelines for Creating a Career Counseling Ministry

Whoever is reading this book needs to pass it on to whoever in your church would be responsible for setting up a career counseling ministry. Share these guidelines with them:

1. Take the idea to the appropriate staff people, including the pastor. For the program to succeed, pastors need to be promoters and cheerleaders of this ministry.
2. Explore how career counseling ministry fits into the mission and program of your church. Would it be under Christian education? youth ministry? young adult ministry? If the church has a mentor program, how might it connect with career counseling?
3. Decide how to promote the program. How will you pitch it to youth and/or young adults?
   - Become familiar with the key concepts discussed earlier in this chapter.
   - Let people know that the purpose of the career counseling group is to do more than help young people figure out what they want to be when they grow up. You may hear, "I already know what I want to be, so I don't need this." Be ready to explain the concepts in this program.
   - Talk about the sessions as a journey of discovery with a group of people who help each other discover their interests, gifts, skills, and ways of thinking about and experiencing God.
   - Mention that participants will gain experience talking about themselves, which is helpful for job and school interviews, writing résumés, and developing social skills.
   - Talk about the vision of having a group in which leaders and group members listen and care and together grow in faith.

4. For youth, arrange to introduce career counseling ministry at a youth group meeting. Plan an hour program, using two of the exercises (that is, "Values and Lifestyle," p. 90, and "Risk Taking, " p. 91) and two or three "Questions of the Day," p. 3 of the journal (see appendix 1). Talk about the key concepts and the process. Share topics from the journal.

   Once youth participants have completed the program, arrange for them to share their experiences with the youth group.
5. Make plans for publicizing career counseling ministry to the entire congregation. Let people know you offer it. It can become a selling point to prospective members who may choose your church specifically because of this ministry.
6. Decide who will be responsible for setting up the program. The leader needs to be someone who has passion for this ministry. We believe you'll find a number of people who, first of all, want to keep youth and young adults from leaving the church and, second, would like to help those who are struggling with vocational questions. These potential leaders will be pleased to know that this program, designed to be led by laypeople, is available.
7. Make plans for the perpetuity of this ministry. It's wise to think now about how to keep the ministry going. First, remember *it takes three years for a new ministry or program to take hold.* So don't throw in the towel if results in the first year seem weak. Evaluate. Decide where changes need to be made. Over time, those who have benefited from the program will be the best ones to promote it and keep it going. In addition, they will be an excellent source for potential mentors and leaders.

CHAPTER 5

Involving Parents, Stepparents, and Guardians

As people who are joined to the body of Christ, we are called to an expression of domestic life that reflects God's love, just as we are called to reflect that love in the whole of our lives.[1]

Those who parent are called to reflect God's unconditional love, to affirm their daughters and sons, and to nurture the unique gifts that God has given their children. The family, in whatever way it's configured, is the setting where values are taught and caught. Family is where faith is formed and practiced, both intentionally and informally. Parents are in a position to model grace, goodness, generosity, forgiveness, service, hospitality, and faithfulness. By observing and living with this modeling, children learn what it means to live a Christian lifestyle.

Providing such a setting of family life is a daily challenge for all who are assigned the role and responsibilities of "parent." Watching children grow and become independent adults can be rough on parents, stepparents, grandparents, guardians, whoever plays the parent role. It's hard seeing your child frustrated or paralyzed by indecision or a lack of direction. It's especially hard when a dilemma immobilizes your son or daughter for months. Those who parent wish they knew how to help effectively. Parents walk a fine line between offering advice and pulling back to let the teenager or grown child exercise independence and responsibility.

Good News: The Generation Gap May Be a Thing of the Past!

If we listen to what is said about today's youth and young adults, we have reason to be optimistic about the relationship between parents and their youth and young adult children. According to generational studies, the generation gap has narrowed significantly. Since today's parents are better educated than those of previous generations, they are closer in educational experience to their children. The rise in the number of women in the work field narrows the experiential gap between mothers and daughters as they face increasingly many of the same lifestyle issues. Young people are more aware of and better understand their families' economic situations than in previous generations. Many have seen parents lose their jobs, and they recognize the toll that such a hardship takes on families.

The millennial generation (those born in 1983 and later) are likely to have many of the same values as their parents. This may come as a surprise, but, according to demographer Susan Mitchell, a 1993 *Good Housekeeping* magazine and Roper Starch Worldwide study found that "parents' opinions matter most to [millennial children] when it comes to drinking, spending money, and questions about sex and AIDS. They even listen more to their parents than their friends about which snack foods to eat."[2]

Other kinds of distances seem to be shrinking as well. Parents and their young people often enjoy the same music. That was unheard of a generation ago. The media have become more explicit in their coverage of such issues as sexuality, drugs, crime, violence, and abuse. What is noteworthy is that parents and teenagers are talking about these subjects more than they did in previous generations. Moreover, studies show that parents matter to their children. According to Ellen Galinsky, writer and researcher on work-family issues, what older kids want is "hanging out time" and "focus time" with parents. "What really matters is when they feel like they can connect."[3]

Parents as Partners

Parents and guardians often feel that if they weren't the "parent," they'd have a better chance of helping their children. Therefore, for the purpose of career counseling, we suggest that parents consider taking on a new role with their youth and young adult children: the role of partner. Being partners brings a level of equality to the parent-child relationship that may never have existed before. Partnership implies a shift from authority figure and advice giver to colleague and listener on the journey of discovery. As partners, parent and child can explore together what God is calling them—both parent and child—to be and do.

Switching from parent to partner is not always easy. When you're a parent, you have a lot invested in your child's life and future. To be a partner involves a change in approach and attitude, which takes determination and practice. The first step is recognizing the difference between the parent approach and the partner approach.

In the parent approach, parents and guardians often assess their child's career prospects in light of their own experience. For example, if the parent gave up a dream vocation in favor of a "steady job," she or he often is less likely to encourage the child to dream. Or if the parent had trouble getting a job because she or he majored in philosophy, the parent may advise offspring to major in a "more practical" field, business or education, for example, so that the child can "always make a living." If working in the family business was good enough for the parent, then the parent may think it should be good enough for the next generation.

In the parent role, parents often assume the position that "parents know best." They tell their children what to do and make decisions for them. They do more talking than listening. Their well-intended comments often lead to arguments. And arguments usually mean no one is listening to anybody. When youth and young adult children sense they are getting nowhere in a conversation with a parent, they tune out.

Wouldn't it be better to be a partner? In the partner approach, parents and guardians step out of the role of "emotionally attached" family member and into a more objective friend-and-ally role. Parents make every effort to shed their biases in order to concentrate on listening to and learning about their children's dreams, interests, values, and fears. As partners, the youth or young adult child and parent walk side by side on the journey of discovery. As partners in the career program, they discuss session activities and what they've learned.

We have found that the concept of parents as partners works with both age groups, youth and young adults. Those young people who have parents who already are good listeners respond eagerly to having parents involved in the career program. They look forward to sharing activities and conversations from the sessions. Other youth are not that eager, for they fear their parents will dominate, preach, or in some way ruin their group experience. But when young people are assured that the activities involving parents are designed to encourage partnership, that parents are advised to listen and not preach, they are more receptive.

Partnership is an ideal relationship for young adults and their parents. The time when the young adult leaves home for college or work is a perfect time to make a shift in the parenting relationship, as leaving home is one of the passages signaling "adulthood." Some young adults readily welcome parents as partners, for they have already experienced parental support in their explorations and struggles. Many other young adults, however, feel the need to push away from family and show parents that they can make it on their own. What these young adults need to know is they aren't supposed to "have their act together" just because they've attained official (chronologically speaking) adulthood.

Often parents of young adults do not live in the same town as their children. These parents can still play the partner role by discussing with their sons and daughters the learnings and activities from the career sessions. Even though they cannot attend a parent session, these parents can communicate with their children by e-mail, chat rooms, telephone, and letters.

Parents and Practices of Faith

As partners, parents and their youth or young adult children explore the many practices of faith and learn from each other. They discuss ways in which they can practice faith, and together they choose the practices they want to try. Then they practice—they pray, meditate, worship, have devotions or Bible study, serve, forgive, practice hospitality or simplicity, whatever practices they choose to explore. Families who are new to particular practices may have difficulty being open to one another and to God. They may not be comfortable talking about their needs and struggles. To engage in practices as a family requires a certain vulnerability, a willingness to show weaknesses, when both parents and their youth and adult children would rather everyone think they are "in control."

Approaching practices as partners helps diminish some of the awkwardness that parents and their older children may feel at first. Partnership implies both parties have ownership of the idea to explore practices. Otherwise, parent or child could reluctantly come to the experience saying, "Remember, this was *your* idea." Partnership levels the playing field and enables parent and child to be equally vulnerable and equally open to the working of the Spirit.

Once families break the ice in the area of spiritual growth and practices of faith, there is the possibility of transformation of the parent-child relationship, for then parent and child see themselves as equal in the sight of God. They see themselves as beloved children, both in need of God's grace, forgiveness, and guidance. Then it is possible for parent and teenage or adult child to grow in faith as they listen for the voice of God in their lives.

Creating Memories: A Practice of Faith

We place this practice in the chapter on parents, instead of in the chapter on practices of faith, because of its special significance for families.

My daughter had three best friends during high school. When they graduated, they decided to collect memorabilia for a time capsule, which they would bury and open twenty years later. We parents, thinking it was a great idea, had a celebration dinner at which the items were shared, put in a large shoe box, wrapped in plastic, and buried in the woods behind one girl's house. That was five years ago. The significance of the event is not the time capsule, which may not survive earthly elements, should we even be able to locate the burial site. Rather, its significance is in the memory created. We all will remember the fun we had that night going through pictures and trinkets that were special to the girls, and the tears we shared when we cut the cake that sported the colors and logos of the four colleges, which marked the girls going their separate ways.

We will never forget that night. It was the first time that all the parents and daughters had shared a meal. It was a time of equal importance to both generations.

The time capsule and all its treasures may be gone, but the memory of that event is the real treasure. This experience brought home to me the significance of creating memories that can be shared within families and within the family of faith.

Creating memories is a practice of faith, one of the oldest, dating back to the Israelites. In the time of Moses, the Lord instituted feasts, Passover being the most familiar, to help people remember what God had done for them. Each year at these feasts, the Jews were to tell their children the story of God's great works. Today, families have opportunities to tell their children stories of faith, both the stories that have been shared in the community of faith and those unique to each family.

From this practice we learn how to pass on our values and traditions, for by creating memories, we share what's important to us and to our families. Memories are a part of our story of faith. Through a practice that started with Moses and culminates in Jesus saying, "Do this in remembrance of me," at the Last Supper, God calls us to remember, to remember who we are and whose we are.

Parent Partners and the Career Counseling Program

Part of the ministry of this career counseling program is to offer tools for families, especially parents and their youth and young adult children, to grow in relationship with God and with one another. This program is a relational ministry that offers a variety of relationships for the participants—relationships with mentors, significant adult friends in the church, workers, employers, and leaders. Therefore, it is crucial that steps be taken to nurture relationships with the most obvious, the most available, and the most interested adults in the youth or young adult's life—parents, stepparents, grandparents, or guardians.

Involving Parents

Leaders of the career counseling ministry program need to consider the necessary steps they should take in connecting with those who parent the youth or young adult participants:

- Find out who plays the parent role for each participant and let that person know what the church offers in career counseling ministry. Include noncustodial parents. Begin by getting correct names and addresses.
- Let parents know that the church supports their work as parents and desires to help them in nurturing their youth and young adult children.
- Be able to explain the career counseling process, the key concepts, the nature of the group, and the sessions. Explain that participants can share parts of the sessions with parents.
- Be able to explain God's call and practices of faith. See chapters 2 and 3.
- Suggest that, during the career counseling journey, parents/guardians reflect on their own faith, work, and lifestyle issues. They can share insights with their children.
- Conduct a parent/guardian session at the beginning of the career counseling process. Hold a parent and participant session during the process. A description of these sessions follows.

Parent/Guardian Session

90 Minutes

This session is designed for those who parent the youth or young adult participants in the career coun-seling process. It takes place at the beginning of the process, before participants begin meeting. Leaders of the career counseling ministry program should lead this session.

Overview

The purpose of this session is:

1. to share the Christian understanding of God's call to lifestyle and vocation (see chapter 3);
2. to introduce parents and guardians to career counseling ministry, giving them a taste of the various activities;
3. to support parents and guardians in the role of partner on this journey of discovery, encouraging them to join their children in seeking to be who God has called them to be and to do what God has called them to do.

Preparation

Make copies of the "Tips for Parents" handout (p. 46) for each parent.
You'll need:

    handout
    8 x 11 paper for each person
    pencils
    candle or cross

The Session

1. Open with Prayer

2. Question of the Day

Begin by making sure people know each other. Invite people to introduce themselves individually, name their sons and daughters, and answer the question of the day (which is also asked in the participants' first session): "When you were a kid, what was something you hoped to be when you grew up?"

3. Key Concepts, Expectations, and Process

Review the key concepts, expectations, and process of the career counseling program. See chapter 8, session 1, number 4 (p. 69) for instructions.

4. God's Call

The challenge facing youth, young adults, and parents is to think theologically about faith, vocation, and lifestyle. Begin discussing God's call by asking: What does it mean to be called by God? Invite parents to share times and situations in which they have felt God calling. Ask: What does it mean that God calls us to a lifestyle and a vocation? Refer to chapter 2 for a discussion of God's call.

5. Inviting God into the Conversation

Begin by asking: How do we find out what God wants us to be and do? Share the career ministry plans to explore with youth or young adults the various ways in which we listen for God. Talk about the concept of inviting God into the conversation. Encourage parents to take on the role of partners and be willing to explore faith practices with their daughters and sons. Encourage parents to do more listening than talking. (See chapter 3 for a discussion of practices of faith.)

6. Sample of Activities from the Sessions

Explain to parents how the sessions will proceed: throughout the six sessions, their sons and daughters will be filling out forms, writing in a journal, talking and listening, giving one another feedback, all in an effort to learn more about themselves, God, work, and life. Then, invite the parents to share the experience. The three exercises that follow are similar to those in the participants' sessions.

- *Exercise 1—Dreaming about the future:* Tell the parents that in the participant's journal is a page titled "Dreaming about the Future." On this page, the youth or young adults will list (and draw) things that they hope will be a part of their lives in the future.
  Hand out paper and pencils. Have the parents list and draw things that they hope will be a part of their lives in the future. Invite them to share answers to the following question: What do you discover about yourself as you look at your list and drawings?
- *Exercise 2—Skills and experiences:* The youth or young adults will be working on a skills inventory and answering the question from their journals: "What skills do you have, things you can do, that someone else might pay you to teach them?"
  Instruct the parents to turn their papers over. On the top half of the paper, they are to answer the same question: What skills do you have, things you can do, that someone else might pay you to teach them? Invite them to share their answers.
- *Exercise 3—Passions:* On the bottom half of the paper, have the parents write thoughts in response to these questions: What do you like about your life right now? What excites you? What are you passionate about? After they have finished, ask: Looking at your dreams, passions, and skills, what do you learn about yourself? Do any of you see a new vocation?

7. Tips for Parents

Distribute the "Tips for Parents" handout (p. 46). Allow time for parents to read the tips, then discuss them. Ask parents which tips capture their attention. Which tip would they like to explore further? Let parents identify the important issues.

8. Questions

Invite parents to raise questions and concerns about the program. Ask for group feedback as you discuss them.

9. Closing

Gather in a circle. Place a candle or cross in the center of the group. Lead the parents in a responsive prayer. Invite them to respond after each request or concern with a phrase such as "For your generous love and continuing guidance, we praise you, gracious God."

Parent/Guardian and Participant Session

90 Minutes

This session is for the youth or young adult participants and their parents, stepparents, grandparents, or guardians. It can be scheduled at any point in the career counseling process after the participants' first session. It does not have to take place between any particular sessions. As with the parent session, the career counseling leader should lead this session.

Overview

The purpose of this session is:

1. to give parents and their youth or young adult children an opportunity to enjoy being together and to get to know more about one another;

2. to give parents and children practice in talking with one another about the journey of seeking God's call to lifestyle and vocation;

3. to look at the world of work and discover interests related to vocation.

Preparation

Make copies of:

the "Parent Questionnaire" (p. 47), one for each parent

the "Participant Questionnaire" (p. 48), one for each participant

the "Occupations" sheet (p. 96), one for each person

the "Occupational Map" (p. 97), one for each person

You'll need:

handouts
pencils
candle or cross

The Session

1. Open with Prayer

2. Question of the Day

Invite all to give their names, one by one; tell where they were on Tuesday morning; and answer the question of the day (from the participants' third session): "What two adjectives would you use to describe yourself?"

3. "Parent Questionnaire" and "Participant Questionnaire"

Distribute the "Parent Questionnaire" to the parents and the "Participant Questionnaire" to the young people and young adults. Invite everyone to gather in family groups. Everyone will spend a few minutes writing answers on their questionnaires, without sharing information or answers. In other words, parents and participants will be guessing some of the answers about each other. If more than one parent or guardian is present from a family, each one fills out a questionnaire. After completing the questionnaires, family members share answers within their family groups.

4. Journey of Seeking God's Call to Lifestyle and Vocation

In session 1, the participants worked on "My Life Line," an exercise that helped them gain perspective on life both past and future. Group members were to share this experience with parents or guardians by asking them to do the exercise. Now, bring everyone together to share their discoveries from that experience. Ask:

• What did you discover about yourself?
• Where has God been present in your life?

5. Occupational Map

Distribute the "Occupations" sheet and the "Occupational Map" sheet.

Invite all to circle the eight occupations on the "Occupations" sheet that they think they would most enjoy. They must circle eight, even if they don't really like eight particular activities. Next, they are to complete the "Occupational Map," following the instructions on the sheet. Tell them to note where the skills categories (People, Data, Ideas, and Things) are positioned on the circle.

When they have finished, ask everyone to share with the group answers to the following questions:

• In which of the six job clusters did you have the most activities circled? which second most? which third?
• Are these job clusters next to each other? (Most likely they will be, although occasionally someone will have a wide variety of interests.)
• Which skills category (People, Data, Ideas, or Things) is related to your cluster(s)?
• What have you discovered about yourself from this?

(Participants are scheduled to do this exercise in session 5. If the parent-participant session takes place before session 5, then having participants work on this exercise alongside parents can strengthen the role of parents as partners. You will still discuss this activity as part of session 5.)

6. Check-In

This session gives participants and parents an opportunity to check in on the progress of the career counseling process. This is a time to discuss and ask questions about informational interviews, job site visits, mentors, careers, God's call, and practices of faith. Participants and parents can share discoveries they have made.

7. Inviting God into the Conversation

In the sessions, participants share their experiences of developing practices of faith. They decide the form of prayer they will use to close each session. Place the candle or cross in the center of the group as a symbol of the light of Christ or the extreme love of God in Jesus Christ. Close with prayer or a practice that the youth or young adults have used in one of their group's closings.

Summary

Those who parent play an incredibly important role in their children's development of faith and values. Our call as the church is to support and nurture them in this role. Involving parents in career counseling ministry may be just the right move at the right time, enabling parents and their youth or young adult children to connect, especially if the parent can take on the role of partner. When parents become partners, they become adults with experience who are willing to explore issues of faith, work, and life with a youth or young adult member of the congregation who happens to be their child. When parents become partners, young adults find a trusted friend who will always be there for them. Partnership opens the door to a whole new way of relating that can last a lifetime.

Tips for Parents

1. *Encourage independence.* Teach decision making. Always keep this advice in mind:

> The extent to which our independence was nurtured in childhood has a big effect on our ability to think and act for ourselves, in any context. Young people are helped toward entrepreneurial thinking when parents applaud their efforts to strike out on their own.[4]

2. *Think of yourself as a partner in your young person's career exploration.*

3. *Be a good listener.* If youth and young adults believe parents really will listen (without judging or advice giving), they are more likely to talk.

4. *Learn to ask open-ended questions.* For instance, instead of asking, "Do you like your class?" which elicits a simple yes or no answer, ask, "What do you like about your class?"

5. *Encourage problem solving.* Play "What if?". This is a learning tool used by parents with children of all ages—often on car trips. Think of a situation and ask your young person, "What would you do if . . . ?" Examples:

- What would you do if you heard someone entering your house?
- In a job interview, what would you do if you were asked what salary you'd accept?
- What would you do if someone told you to lie to your employer?

6. *Talk about people's vocations.* Introduce your daughter or son to people who have careers, values, or lifestyles that may interest them.

7. *Be a fellow learner.* Listen when your youth or young adult shares discoveries about God's call, life, faith, the world of work, and themselves. Let them teach you.

8. *Model values.* Talk about your values. Studies show that children develop their values at home and are likely to adopt the values of their parents. Pass on values without passing on your judgments or prejudices about people and jobs. Encourage the development of your child's individuality.

9. *Examine the way you talk about your job.* For example, do you often say you dread going to work? Do you talk about nailing your competition or how you avoided extra work? If you do, you may be giving your children an impression of your work-related values that either may not be accurate or may not be what you want them to have.

10. *Teach social skills.* Give children opportunities to be with adults and include them in conversations with adults. Youth and young adults who are comfortable being around adults have an easier time networking and interviewing.

11. *Encourage relationships with mentors.* Your sons and daughters need adults—in addition to parents—who can become significant adult friends.

Parent Questionnaire

1. As a child, something your son or daughter wanted to be when he or she grew up _____
_____

2. Your child's favorite thing to do on a Saturday _____

3. Something your child does well _____

4. A talent your child has _____

5. Your child's favorite teacher _____

6. Someone your child admires _____

7. Someone your child considers a role model _____

8. Someone whose job you think your child would love to have _____

9. An issue about which your child has strong feelings _____

10. Where you think your child would like to live _____
_____

11. Something your child could teach someone else to do _____
_____

12. Something about your daughter or son that makes you proud _____
_____

Participant Questionnaire

1. Something your parent wanted to be when he or she grew up _____

_____

2. Your parent's favorite thing to do on a Saturday _____

_____

3. Something your parent does well _____

4. A talent your parent has _____

5. Your parent's first job _____

6. Someone who is or was your parent's mentor _____

7. Someone your parent would consider a role model _____

8. Someone whose job you think your parent would love to have _____

_____

9. An issue about which your parent has strong feelings _____

10. Where you think your parent would like to live _____

11. Something your parent could teach someone else to do _____

12. Something about your parent that makes you proud _____

_____

Chapter 6

Mentors

As we wrote this chapter, the Columbine High School shootings in Littleton, Colorado, reminded us again of the horror of children killing children. More than ever before, people are looking for solutions to the problem. How can we stop the violence? Of course, there are no easy answers. But what if every child had just one person who cares, who thinks that the child is special; one person who will listen. What if every child had a mentor?

Many adults know the value of having a mentor, someone who took an interest in them, perhaps encouraged them at a particular point in their lives. Or perhaps the mentor showed them the ropes of whatever career they pursued. Or perhaps it was someone who shared her or his life experiences and words of wisdom. Or maybe it was someone who just listened.

If you think you never had a mentor, listen to what people say about their mentors and see if any of their words resonate with your experience:

> Because of her, I have the confidence that I can do anything I put my mind to.
> He treated me with respect.
> She made me feel good about myself.
> He was there for me.
> She helped me to know God.
> His door was always open.

> She encouraged me to be proud of who I was.
> She helped me to see consequences, cause and effect.
> He helped me understand my responsibility to care for other people.
> He taught me that failure was a gift.
> She believed in me when I didn't believe in myself.
> He told me I had talent that I didn't know I had.
> She was a role model, an inspiration, and a good friend.
> He taught me the value of making the other guy look good.
> He told me I was on the right track in my thinking about faith and God.
> She taught me how to connect my faith and my work.
> She showed me how important it was to be accountable.
> He was a model of how to live as a Christian.
> He never gave up on me.

Teenagers and young adults often lack confidence in their abilities, their ideas, and their beliefs. To have someone affirm their abilities and beliefs or just tell them they are on the right track has a powerful impact on their self-esteem. It is a huge boost to their self-confidence to have just one person think highly of them, to tell them they are capable.

What Is a Mentor?

In Greek mythology, Mentor was the name of the person who served as guardian, teacher, and companion to Ulysses' son, Telemachus, while Ulysses was off on his adventures. The name has continued through the centuries to refer to people who take special interest in the development of a person's education, vocation, faith, lifestyle, and/or well-being. Vocational mentors were common in the early days of industrialization, as people learned their trade by serving as apprentices to masters.

A mentor is a person who cares, guides, directs, teaches, challenges, goes to bat for, shares skills with, listens to, models, advises, encourages, and inspires. Mentors share their stories, journeys, faith, values, questions, struggles, roadblocks, triumphs, transitions, and learnings with those they befriend and counsel. Mentors point out options and help put things into perspective. They point to resources and connections that will help those they mentor in their lifestyle and vocation.

Having a mentor in faith is a gift from God. Such mentors help people work through their understandings of God, their faith experiences, and their beliefs. By sharing their own faith journeys and struggles, these mentors model a lifestyle of faith as a work in progress. Mentors engage mentorees in conversations about practices of faith, faith and work, living as a Christian, discerning God's call, and making decisions. The one mentored is not the only one who benefits. Mentors learn from their mentorees. It is a relationship, a partnership on a journey to grow in faith.

Some people have mentors who serve specifically as spiritual directors or spiritual friends. The relationship is formed for the purpose of nurturing spiritual growth and creating time and space for cultivating the practices of faith. Some spiritual retreat sites offer spiritual directors who meet regularly with those on retreat.

Mentoring can take place in groups. A youth ministry in a Houston church has an interesting mentor program. An adult male layperson meets with a group of six boys, and a female adult with a group of girls. These groups meet one hour before their regular Sunday-night youth meeting. A junior boy reports: "We just talk about whatever's on our minds. Our mentor really cares about us. He's someone I trust. I can tell him things I don't feel I can tell my parents. But because of his guidance I'm getting better at talking with my parents. What's special about our group is that we hold each other accountable." In much the same way, mentoring can occur in the career counseling groups. The leaders can serve as mentors to the participants.

Mentors in the Bible

Several mentor relationships can be found in the Bible. In the career counseling sessions, the participants will look at two such relationships from the Old Testament: the one between Eli and Samuel and the one between Naomi and Ruth. Samuel was dedicated to the Lord by his mother, Hannah, and given to Eli, the priest, to be raised. We can recognize Eli's role as mentor in 1 Samuel 3, which recounts God's call to Samuel. It was Eli who realized the voice was God's and instructed Samuel to listen.

Naomi (who was from Israel) guided her daughter-in-law Ruth (from Moab, an enemy of Israel) in her work, faith, and relationships. Ruth pledged utmost loyalty to Naomi and to God, as we see her say to Naomi in Ruth 1:16: "Where you go, I will go. . . . Your

people shall be my people, and your God my God."

Other examples of biblical mentor relationships occur between Moses and Joshua, Elijah and Elisha, Paul and Timothy, and, the best example of mentoring, Jesus and his disciples. The mentor relationship between Jesus and Peter is particularly interesting. Jesus saw Peter's potential and affirmed him, saying, "On this rock I will build my church" (Matthew 16:18). Jesus challenged him but also admonished him, particularly when Peter rebuked Jesus for predicting Jesus' suffering and death (Matthew 16:21–23). Jesus never gave up on Peter. Even after Peter denied Christ three times, Jesus welcomed him back into ministry with three parallel statements of the commission "Feed my sheep" (John 21:15–19).

Mentors in Career Counseling Ministry

In career counseling ministry, a mentor is a member of the congregation who is willing to take interest in a young person or young adult who is participating in the career counseling program. The mentor must be a member of the congregation, because to be most effec-

tive, this program must be a ministry of the local church. Mentors can be found elsewhere, of course, and participants may connect with people outside the church as they explore career fields, but we recommend exploring the possibilities within the congregation first.

We hope that participants will establish a mentor relationship during this program and keep the relationship for years. But things don't always work that way. Many of the people I consider my mentors are people whose words or actions at a particular point in my life made an impact on my life. Participants may find several mentors like this, people with whom they may or may not develop a long-term relationship.

Some churches already have mentor programs in place. Often the programs are tied to confirmation. When young people enter the confirmation process, they are assigned a mentor or elder partner, often a member of the congregation's governing body. A career counseling mentor program may branch off from an existing mentor program.

Benefits of a Mentor Program

Developing a mentor program takes a lot of work, planning, and communication, but there are many benefits for many people.

The Participants Benefit by:
- getting to know a church member who has experience in life, work, and faith;
- having someone to talk to who cares and listens, who can serve as a sounding board as they ponder decisions and steps to take on the journey of faith and vocation;
- having a significant adult friend who will encourage, challenge, support, and offer connections to resources.

Mentors Benefit by:
- being a part of an important ministry of the church;
- helping a young person or young adult;

- engaging in challenging conversations about faith, life, and work;
- growing in their own faith.

The Church Benefits by:
- offering a distinctive ministry to young adults, youth, singles, whoever is the focus group;
- connecting people of different generations;
- giving people opportunities to practice talking about their faith journeys.

Parents and Guardians Benefit by:
- knowing there is someone who cares specifically about their son or daughter;
- having a nonfamily person who is willing to talk with their sons and daughters about faith, life, and work;
- knowing that the mentor is encouraging communication between the participant and the family.

Structure of the Mentor Program

In the career counseling mentor program, the mentor arranges to meet with the participant weekly for three months. Meetings can be at the mentor's home, at a restaurant for lunch or for a coke, or at the church. Meetings can also be outings, to visit schools, a business, a military base, a ball game, whatever. Many have found shopping malls a relaxed place to talk and build relationships. Mentors can invite those they mentor to dinner or to their workplace. They can arrange visits to other workplaces. Through their mentors, participants can meet others who can share stories of career search experiences or of discerning their call.

The first meeting of mentors and their mentorees can be at the church or in a home. Get-acquainted activities can serve as icebreakers to help the two peo-

ple get over the jitters of a first meeting; yes, mentors can be nervous too.

At the second meeting, we recommend that each mentor and mentoree draw up a simple covenant, which we explain under the guidelines below.

Over the course of their time together, mentors share career journeys; they talk about the doors that opened and the ones that closed, the exciting turning points, and the barriers and challenges. They also share their faith journeys, the times that God was especially present, the times of questioning and struggling with faith. Both parties can share experiences of establishing practices of faith. Many mentors and mentorees become prayer partners. Mentorees can share exercises and discussions from the career sessions. They can work together on a service project or other ministry in the church.

At the end of the three-month period, the mentor and participant should take a break and schedule to meet in a month to decide the future of the relationship.

Guidelines for Career Counseling Mentor Programs

As with other mentor programs, there is no one right way to design a career counseling mentor program. We offer ideas here and encourage you to adapt them to the situation in your church.

A few guidelines will help you get started and succeed:

1. *Set a time limit for the mentor relationship.* Three months of weekly meetings have proven a good model. It encourages frequent contact so that a relationship can be established, without asking too much of either party. Setting an end date frees both parties from staying in a commitment that may not be working. Ideally, after a break, the relationship will continue, though the parties may see each other only occasionally.

    A friend of mine has had a mentor for thirty-five years yet sees him only once every few years. When they get together, they pick up right where they left off. Every time they meet, the mentor offers insights and asks challenging questions, which leads my friend into periods of reflection, prayer, and study, from which he makes significant decisions about what God is calling him to do next.

2. *Invite prospective mentors by calling them to serve God in this particular ministry.* Help them see that, should they choose to accept, they are responding to God's call to serve. Assure them that it will be mutually beneficial. Both mentors and mentorees grow in faith and understanding as together they explore issues of God's call, career, and lifestyle.

3. *Emphasize commitment.* Commitment is that scary word, especially among volunteers. Stressing commmitment assures the mentors that what they are doing is of utmost importance. Commitment is necessary, or a participant could be let down.

4. *Encourage covenant writing.* Covenants can help the concern about commitment. To write a covenant, mentor and mentoree discuss what they want from the relationship and create a few statements of what they are willing to do, for instance, listen, be honest, respect opinions, respect the right not to answer, keep confidences, share the experience with families (except for confidences, of course), encourage each other, and pray. The time commitment and type of activities could be included. Covenant writing encourages both parties to be candid and gives them permission at any time to bring up an issue that is breaking the covenant.

5. *Encourage mentors to share their faith journeys, their experiences of God, and their struggles.* We caution mentors not to preach or feel the need to indoctrinate those they mentor. Mentorees learn best through inquiry and exploration. It helps to approach the relationship with a listening ear and a desire to learn.

6. *Encourage mentors and mentorees to explore the practices of faith together, both in discussion and in practice.* Praying together can be a bonding experience.

7. *Insist on a break after three months, even if the mentor relationship is successful.* After time off, the mentor and mentoree can meet and redefine the relationship, deciding whether or not to continue meeting regularly. They can identify upcoming events involving big decisions, or they might do a mission or other church project together. Explore the possibilities.

Setting Up the Mentor Program

A mentor program can become a vital ministry of your church, as it connects youth and young adults with caring members of their congregations. Therefore, you need to plan carefully how to proceed. Whoever is responsible for implementing the career counseling ministry program needs to talk with the pastor, staff, and leaders of youth or young adult ministry to decide how to do the program. It may be wise to concentrate on setting up the six career counseling sessions the first year and work toward adding the mentor component the second year.

In our churches, we have had some challenges when trying to launch mentor programs. The major challenge is recognizing that it takes time and effort and someone diligent to oversee the program. We have learned a number of things from our experiences and mistakes:

- Start early. Let the congregation know you are looking for mentors. Publicize the mentor program, explaining its place in career counseling ministry.
- Form a mentor program planning group that will take responsibility for overseeing and perpetuating mentoring. That group may consist of the career counseling leaders, a leader of youth or young adults, a teenager or young adult, a parent, a person in the counseling or career counseling field. This group would:

1. discuss the program and its key concepts;
2. review and adapt the job description of mentors and mentorees;
3. identify potential mentors;
4. explore ways to match mentors and mentorees;
5. plan the orientation and the first meeting of mentors and mentorees and decide who is to lead each;
6. suggest possible activities for mentors and mentorees to do together;
7. promote the program;
8. evaluate the program and make needed changes.

Finding Mentors

Since youth or young adults may find it difficult or intimidating to ask someone to be their mentor, we suggest that each participant in the program list several people they would like as mentors and give the names to the leaders. The leaders would then inform these people, by phone or in person, that a participant has requested them as mentors for a period of three months as part of the career counseling process. Most people are flattered that someone regards them as mentor material.

Young people or young adults usually request individuals whom they admire, or people who have careers in a field in which they have interest, or someone whose lifestyle or faith commitment they admire. The prospective mentor may be involved in a ministry or service project that appeals to the participant.

Looking for mentors teaches the participants to become observers of people, which is an important skill for career planning and faith development. Youth and young adults often tend to be so focused on their own concerns that they rarely notice people beyond their own little world. Looking for mentors raises their awareness of the variety of ways in which people live their lives, approach their work, and practice their faith.

Mentor Job Description

The following is a list of expectations that the church has of its mentors.

1. Recognize that service as a mentor is a calling from God.
2. Be willing to give three months of regular weekly meetings with your mentoree. If you need to reschedule a meeting, call the mentoree.
3. Be respectful of young people and young adults.
4. Be willing to initiate contact with the mentoree.
5. Honor the commitment and covenant you make with your mentoree.
6. Be willing to share your faith and your career journey.
7. Be a good listener. In a mentor relationship, listening is more important than advising.
8. Respect various faith experiences, recognizing that people come to faith and grow in faith in a variety of ways and at various paces.
9. Share practices of faith. Pray together.
10. Be open to learning and growing. Mentor relationships are mutually beneficial. Faith grows when it is seen from another's perspective.
11. Be involved in the life of the church.
12. Keep confidences.

Mentoree Job Description

1. View the mentor relationship as part of your call from God to grow in faith and in understanding of God, self, vocation, and lifestyle.
2. Be willing to attend three months of weekly meetings with the mentor. If you need to reschedule a meeting, call the mentor.
3. Honor the relationship and be open to learning from your mentor's life experience.
4. Honor the commitment and covenant you make with your mentor.
5. Be willing to share (a) your faith and career journey; (b) the insights you gain during the career sessions; (c) experiences, struggles, and questions.
6. Listen with the intent to understand your mentor's perspective.
7. Respect the faith experiences of your mentor. At the same time, be assured that your experience is valid, even if it is different from your mentor's.
8. Share practices of faith. Pray together.
9. Be open to learning and growing. Mentor relationships are mutually beneficial. Faith grows when it is seen from another's perspective.
10. Be involved in the life of the church.
11. Keep confidences.

Mentor Orientation

Orientation for mentors needs to take place as soon as mentors have been assigned. The mentor program planning group or the career counseling leader needs to decide who is going to lead the orientation. It could be the career counseling leaders, a pastor or church staff person, or someone who has had experience with mentor relationships.

At the orientation, the leader must:

1. Explain the career counseling process. Provide an overview of the sessions, and discuss the importance of the journal and participant activities.
2. Review the key concepts of the career counseling ministry. See chapter 4, p. 32, and page 1 in the journal (appendix 1).
3. Review and discuss the mentor job description.
4. Discuss faith issues that may arise in a mentoring relationship. Review the variety of ways in which young people and young adults come to faith and grow in faith. (For resources on faith development, see appendix 3.) Recognize that those being mentored may have challenging questions or questions that reflect doubting faith, and that mentors should resist the urge to "set them straight." Remind mentors that developing faith goes through stages and needs time, caring understanding, and a willingness to listen. If mentorees feel put down, they are likely to clam up and never raise another issue or question.
5. Discuss the first meeting between mentors and mentorees. Suggest get-acquainted questions, such as those listed below under "The First Meeting." Mentors and mentorees are on their own to set up a schedule for getting together.
6. Give mentors the names of people (leaders or staff) they can call, should they have questions or encounter problems.

The First Meeting of Mentors and Mentorees

Even if there are only two participants in the career counseling process, getting all the mentors and mentorees together is the best way to begin a mentor relationship. Since meeting someone for the first time is a little awkward, and since expectations of mentors and mentorees may be high, a crowd is welcome, no matter how small.

This meeting should last no longer than ninety minutes and can be led by the same person who led the mentor orientation. Begin with an arrival activity, such as making creative name tags. Participants should write their names at the top of a half sheet of construction paper. Under their names, they may then draw symbols representing five of their interests or hobbies; they may list adjectives that describe themselves; or they may do an acrostic name tag, writing their first name down the left side of the paper and for each letter of their name write a word that tells something about themselves.

Gather as one group for introductions. Each person gives his or her name, school or job, and one little-known fact about himself or herself. After some general announcements and details about the mentor program and the career counseling process, invite the mentors and mentorees to spend the rest of the time in mentor pairs, sharing answers to questions that are designed to provide personal information in a noninvasive way, such as those listed below. For additional questions, see page 3 in the journal, which lists the question of the day from each session.

Break-the-Ice Questions

From the list below, choose a question to ask. The mentor pairs have five minutes to talk with each other about that question, each giving the other an answer. The leader should call time and then ask the next question. Both mentor and mentoree should answer the question. Sometimes, in new situations, one partner will do all the talking.

1. Name a movie you've seen recently, and tell why you liked or didn't like it.
2. If you could have dinner with two famous people, who would you choose and why?
3. Complete this sentence any way you wish: I grew up in a _____ with _____.
4. If you could live somewhere else for a year, where would you live and why?
5. What did you do in the summer when you were a child?
6. What is something you are afraid of?
7. What was church like for you as a child?
8. If you could go somewhere for two weeks to learn about or study something, where would you go and what would you study?
9. At what event, worship service, or activity in our church have you felt closest to God?
10. What was (or is) the hardest thing for you about being a teenager?
11. Describe your dream vacation. What would you be doing and where?
12. What's important to you in life? What do you value?
13. If you could ask God one question, what would it be?
14. Talk about a time when you took a risk, did something that was outside your comfort zone.

Integrating the Mentor Program and Career Counseling Ministry

Matching mentors and mentorees can happen any time during the career counseling process. In your sessions, encourage participants to look for prospective mentors as they conduct their informational interviews. If the first meeting between a participant and a mentor occurs outside the counseling setting, you may not have a first meeting of all mentors and mentorees. In this case, give the list of questions to individual mentor partners at their initial get-together. Remember that these mentors will still need some kind of orientation. Be prepared to meet with them and discuss material from the mentor orientation.

If the group agrees, mentors can be invited to a session. Some group members may feel that adding people, even mentors for a single session, may change the group dynamic. Or they may see it as a good way to include mentors in the career process. Participants who do not have mentors should have a voice in this decision.

Create special events for mentors and mentorees. Have a special meeting or go out to eat. Mentoring can happen in a lot of different environments. Encourage mentor partners to enjoy each other. Also, consider special occasions for mentor partners to meet with parents/guardians, as parents appreciate knowing those special adults who are interested in their children. Since the career counseling process can continue in some form beyond the six sessions, you can be creative with your scheduling, mixing additional career sessions with mentor partnership events and parent/guardian events, trips to schools or job fairs, outings for fun, mission trips.

Integrate some of the career-oriented get-togethers with events in the life of the church. Work with the church staff to coordinate activities and inform the congregation that career ministry is a vital ministry of the church.

Challenges Facing Mentor Programs

As with any new program or ministry in a church, it takes time, lots of effort, and trial and error to get it going. Remember that it takes three years to establish any significant new program or ministry in the local church.

You will face two immediate and potential challenges to success, although no doubt you'll discover others. In one case, the mentor doesn't honor his or her commitment. In the other, the match does not work.

Challenge 1:
The Mentor Doesn't Follow Through.

It is not uncommon for an adult mentor to fail to contact the mentoree. A mentor might say: "I told her to call me any time" or "I've been meaning to, but I just got busy." Even worse is someone who says to you, "I'll call him this week," and then doesn't call.

The best defense, as the adage goes, is a good offense, which is why we stress mentor orientations and covenants. You must clearly state and repeat that the mentor has the responsibility of initiation. The mentor calls the mentoree; it does not work the other way around. Of course, the mentoree can, and in good mentor relationships will, call the mentor. A long-term goal of mentoring is to give the one being mentored someone to call when she or he faces a decision or

problem. Writing a covenant gives the mentor and mentoree an opportunity to talk about expectations and what to do if either party doesn't live up to the expectations.

The mentor program leader or career counseling leader should call the mentor at the first sign of neglect to check on the relationship. Ignoring the situation only makes it harder to make that call. Staying on top of the relationship lets everyone concerned know the mentor relationship is important.

Challenge 2: The Match Is Not Working.

When either mentor or mentoree claims the relationship is not working, you should first listen to the person to try to discover why. Clarifying each person's expectations may correct a problem. Checking the covenant may help. Or it may be that the judgment has been made too soon. Encourage the doubting partner to be open, give the relationship a chance, and continue meeting a few more times.

There are times, however, when a match just doesn't work. In that case, the program leader should ask the other partner how it's going. Both partners may know it's not working, even though only one speaks up. Dissolving the relationship may be the best solution.

Participants Are Responsible for Recognizing Mentors in Life

Participants need to be reminded that there is more than one potential mentor out there. They will have many mentors in life, if they are open to recognizing them. The fifty-nine-year-old woman mentioned at the beginning of chapter 3, who was sure God did not have a plan for her life, also believed her whole life would have been different had she had a mentor. Her hopelessness motivated me to strive to develop opportunities for youth and young adults to have mentors. While working on a mentor program for our congregation, our leadership team realized that our expectations of one mentor for each young person and young adult was a worthy goal but not always a realistic one.

As we learned more about mentoring, we made an important discovery that would have been tragic had we missed it. The truth is, not many of us can point to

a full-scale mentor, someone who pointed the way, nurtured, encouraged, challenged, and did all the things mentors by definition do. Not many of us were apprenticed, as in the old days when apprenticeships were the basic way to learn a trade.

But that doesn't mean we were unmentored and left to figure out life all by ourselves. Rather, when we thought about it, most of us were mentored in one way or another by a lot of people. The problem is, we don't think of the person who in passing said, "You know, you're really good at that," or, "I think you're on the right track," as a mentor, for the simple reason that the encouragement was offered in passing. These people greatly influenced our choices in life by something they said or did at a particular moment, but we didn't quite notice it for what it was.

The "aha" in all this is that we must regularly alert young people and young adults to be aware of the positive, though seemingly inconsequential, things that people do for them and to hear the encouraging words, even if few and far between, that people say to them. One's attitude and approach to life are critical issues here. People who perceive life as miserable, whose basic, gut-level approach to living is negative, *will not be able to perceive or remember the good things or the encouraging words.* They will miss them.

Not everyone who is a part of this career counseling program will end up with a long-term mentor relationship. But some will. Not everyone will "click" with his or her mentor. But some will. Those who don't find a mentor must not despair. They will be mentored in many ways, by their group leaders, by people who show interest in them during informational interviews and on job sites, by pastors, lay leaders, significant adult friends, relatives, teachers, coaches, and heroes (both in person and in print).

Please remind the youth and young adults in your group that the responsibility for having mentors ultimately rests with their ability to recognize them when they appear, no matter how briefly. Mentor finding may be disappointing for some, so they need to think beyond the traditional concept of mentor. They need to be alert, to recognize that anyone they encounter can impact their lives simply with a word or gesture.

Adapting Career Counseling Ministry to Youth and Young Adults with Special Needs

They look at you as disabled, not as thoughtful, kind, and smart.—Young adult with spina bifida

It is altogether likely that your church will have the opportunity to involve youth and young adults with special needs in the career counseling process. Like everyone, these young people and young adults are seeking ways to find their place in the world and to use their gifts and abilities in life. Like everyone, individuals with disabilities are called by God to a life of faithfulness. It is natural, however, for parents, relatives, and friends of a person with a disability to feel anxious about that person's prospects for employment. The church stands in a unique place to work with individuals with special needs through the career counseling ministry program, helping them listen for God, discover their gifts, and discern what God is calling them

to be and do. This chapter is written to help the career counseling leader adapt this program to involve the special-needs person.

A variety of terms have been used to describe those who have a disability—*disabled, handicapped, challenged, special-needs.* We struggle to use the politically correct terms, but these terms change periodically. More important, we need to get beyond labels of any kind. We must first realize that people with disabilities are people, real people with real needs, real feelings, real potential, real hopes, and real dreams. Theologically, we affirm that we are all children of God. Our diversities include our abilities and our disabilities. We are all able and disabled in some way.

Encounter with a Disability

Tina's Story

Tina never thought she'd be where she is now. When she was thirty-five, her car hydroplaned and crashed. She woke up in a Thomasville, Georgia, hospital, surrounded by medical devices. Due to heavy medications, she was not fully aware of her condition. Five weeks later, she was transferred to a hospital in Jacksonville, Florida. Reality hit. Tina was a quadriplegic. She faced physical therapy, medical therapy, occupational therapy, and personal care lessons. She had to learn about medications, dosages, and self-care techniques. "From the moment I wake up, I have to start thinking. You are constantly problem solving, which is exhausting. You can't do anything the way you once did." Seven years after her accident, she is still adapting.

Tina was taught in rehabilitation that you have to take charge of yourself and your environment, and that it's up to you to make others aware. She says, "You are responsible for your care. There is a wrestling with wanting someone to take care of you versus taking care of yourself. There is no rescue. No one can fully know your situation."

While some would sink into despair, Tina continues to look upward. "You get so far down, there isn't any way to look but up." Her faith and God's calling strengthened her. "Help comes from God," she said, as she reflected on what God was calling her to be and do. Tina met Peter Marshall, the director of Project Faith, a local ministry in the Atlanta area, which reaches out to persons with disabilities, helping them discover a new sense of hope. Peter leads stretching exercises and talks and prays with persons with disabilities. Project Faith allows Tina and others to continue to seek God's will for their lives.[1]

Types of Disabilities

Disabilities affect one-fifth of all Americans, and the number of disabled people is growing. Church leaders need to be aware that there are many types of disabilities:

1. physical disabilities, such as a physical impairment that requires a prosthesis or a wheelchair;
2. mental or genetic disabilities, such as emotional or cognitive impairment, Down's syndrome, cerebral palsy, psychoses, or schizophrenia;
3. medical disabilities, such as attention deficit disorder (ADD, ADHD, ADD-Inattentive), sight impairment, hearing impairment, reactions to medications, chronic fatigue syndome, cancer, or viruses.

In recent years, disability awareness programs have educated people about special needs. Churches use these programs and resources with church members of all ages to increase their awareness of various disabilities. In some, members participate in activities that simulate a disability, enabling them, in a limited sense, to experience that particular disability.

Eliminating the Stereotypes

Before we discuss life in the work world for special-needs persons, we need to dispel some of the stereotypes surrounding those who have disabilities. People with disabilities are not inferior or incomplete human beings. They were not put on this earth to serve as someone's "cross to bear." Like everyone else, they have feelings, opinions, and capabilities. They have potential, just as we all do. Persons with disabilities are often ignored by well-meaning people who assume that the disabled person would prefer to be left alone, or that the person is mentally incapable of communication.

Many people have long assumed it would be impractical for people with disabilities to risk venturing out into the world of work and careers. After all, the reasoning goes, their lives are filled with coping and adapting. Why would they want to explore the unpredictable and precarious frontier of work? There are many reasons why. For one thing, if at all possible, everyone prefers to be self-supporting and not on public assistance. Many persons with disabilities can be employed. Many have abilities that are marketable.

Furthermore, like everyone, people with special needs prefer to be seen as persons of worth. Each person has potential and a right to pursue their capabilities. People with special needs want to work because they have hope.

Hope and Employment

Persons with disabilities are more hopeful than ever before that they will be able to use their gifts and abilities in the world of work. There are a number of reasons for their sense of hope. First, the world and attitudes are changing. It is common today to see persons with disabilities at work in almost every profession. Job mentors and coaches are available to work with disabled persons. There are job tasks that focus on abilities well within the capabilities of some disabled persons.

The Americans with Disabilities Act (ADA)[2] provides employers with guidelines for employing persons with disabilities and for making reasonable accommodations to enable them to work. The work world is discovering ways to be more flexible and adaptive. Employers are willing to explore changes in hours, duties, and accessibility. The growth in technology also provides special-needs persons with opportunities to work from their homes. The Independent Homeworkers Association (www.homeworkers.org) is dedicated to serving people who work or want to work from their homes. Furthermore, from a public relations perspective, hiring those with a disability makes a positive statement about a company and its policies.

Elementary schools and high schools have resources to prepare children with various disabilities for life and work. Schools vary in the level of services, however, so parents must do some investigating. For example, when Heather, who has a form of cerebral palsy, was school age, her parents, Dan and Pat, were directed to resources in the public school system, which began for them a long process of learning. "The learning curve is pretty steep and pretty quick," Dan says. Heather entered a special education program with special classes at first. Eventually she was able to participate in general education classes and in regular high school activities.

As part of Heather's career planning, her parents and a team of school officials developed Heather's annual IEP (Individualized Education Program), which called for the continued development of life skills along with community job-related practice. Heather worked in department stores and service industries while continuing her schooling. Pat notes that it was "no accident that Heather found herself in a school system that put so much emphasis on life skills, vocation, and transition from school to work training." God was at work in the process.

Dan and Pat anticipate that someday Heather may find meaningful employment and a supportive living environment, maybe a group home. Because of the continuing collaboration of their church, family, and community, their expectations continue to be high for Heather.

God's Call and Special-Needs Persons

From a theological perspective, the most important reason special-needs people want to venture into the world of work is because they have an inner call to put their God-given abilities to work. Special-needs persons are children of God, who are called by God. It is easy to accept the idea that the physically disabled can be called by God. But is it true as well for those who don't have the mental ability to comprehend such a call? It is impossible for us, in our limited understanding of how God works, to claim that God can work through some people and not through others. Who are we to say that God cannot call or work through the severely disabled? But we can make several affirmations about God's call and persons with special needs:

1. *God calls everyone, including persons with disabilities.* We are all called to be followers of Jesus Christ and to discern what God is calling us to be and to do. In Tina's story, we saw a young woman who, instead of giving in to despair, continues to trust that God is working in her life.

2. *God calls individuals and uses their gifts, often without their knowing it.* Special-needs persons are abled persons in that they have God-given abilities. They can use those abilities in the workplace. They bear witness to God's actions by using their God-given gifts, often without awareness of their impact on the church and community. I recall a Down's syndrome young adult who was a faithful church member. The entire congregation knew she had a special call from God. She regularly referred to my husband, Jim, who was her pastor, as Jim "Cross." Her spirit and certainty mystically confirmed the simple truth of God's love.

3. *God's call comes to entire families.* The families of special-needs persons bear witness to the extraordinary and often surprising faith experiences that occur as a result of having a family member with disabilities. Faith, lives, careers, and lifestyles are transformed as these special-needs family members bring forth faith-filled acts of discipleship.

Some instances are better known than others. Take Jim Kelly, former quarterback of the Buffalo Bills, whose son, Hunter, has Krabbe's disease, a rare genetic disorder. Hunter is unable to speak, swallow, or move on his own. His disability is as severe as it gets. At two and a half, he had outlived his life expectancy by more than a year. To hear Jim and Jill Kelly talk about the blessing that Hunter has been, it is clear that God has called Hunter to play a special role in their lives and in the lives of anyone connected to a Krabbe's diseased baby. God's call has come to the entire Kelly family. They have started Hunter's Hope, a foundation whose goal is to find a cure for Krabbe's. Jim and Jill state clearly their conviction that God has called them to this mission.

4. *God's call comes to entire communities.* In chapter 2, we talk about the we-ness of the call and the way in which the community confirms the call. In many cases it is the community that recognizes how God works through a special-needs person.

At a meeting of the National Council of Churches' Ministries in Education Committee, a pastor told a story about his daughter Amy, who has Down's syndrome. One Sunday during worship, the congregation was asked to submit nominations for elders and deacons. Amy asked her father, "What does a deacon do?" He described the responsibilities—taking care of the church property, visiting church members, greeting people at worship, serving as an usher, among others. Amy thought a few minutes and said, "I could do that."

Amy's name was submitted to the nominating committee. She was nominated and elected to the office of deacon. Amy went through officer training, was examined, and was ordained to serve. The pastor reported that Amy's presence and service have transformed the board of deacons. She serves as a greeter and usher and takes special pride in helping to keep the sanctuary spick-and-span. Other deacons were inspired by her example and have become more caring and compassionate in carrying out their responsibilities. Amy has become a model of how a deacon serves the church.

Adapting the Career Counseling Ministry Program for Special-Needs Persons

As the leader of the career counseling ministry program, you will need to assess on an individual basis the modifications that may need to be made in order to include youth or young adults with special needs. In some cases, with persons with attention deficit disorder, for example, few or no modifications need to be made, as these persons have gained coping skills throughout their educational career.

In other cases, you will need to discuss the program with the special-needs persons. Show them the handouts, which involve reading and writing. They can tell you whether or not they would feel comfortable doing the activities with the group. They can share with you their limitations.

In still other cases, the best approach is to involve the parent or caregiver who is responsible for the special-needs person. Ask them for advice in using this program. Show them the material in the sessions. Describe the activities. Show them the handouts.

You can use the following questions as you consider modifications that may be needed in the program and building:

- Can the special-needs person participate in all the activities?
- How well do the youth or young adults in the church relate to this person?
- What leaders or teachers have had experience with this person? Consult them.
- Are the prospective participants in the career counseling program open to including the person in the sessions' activities and discussions?
- Are there physical limitations that must be addressed, such as the accessibility of the meeting location?
- What are the expectations of the parents or caregivers for this person?
- Is an interpreter or mentor needed to assist this person in the career counseling ministry program?

Career Counseling Ministry in a Family Setting

In some cases, the best option for a special-needs person may be career counseling ministry in a family setting. A family-based setting allows family members to be involved—persons who have known and loved the special-needs individual and who can help identify his or her gifts and talents. The career counseling leader or another mentor can serve as leader in this setting, and weekly meetings in the home can be arranged.

In addition, families of special-needs persons may find these ideas helpful as part of the career counseling experience:

- Seek family members or caregivers of other special-needs persons who have similar disabilities. Share joys and concerns. Consider joining a support group or organization that deals with the particular disability, and explore work-related concerns and ideas.
- Explore the growing wealth of Internet resources related to the special needs of the youth or young adult. Search for educational and employment-related Internet sites for special-needs persons, such as the Mining Company, which has a wealth of resources and links (http://specialchildren.miningco.com).
- Seek out special-needs persons who are employed. These persons can offer guidance on what to expect and how to approach employers. The Americans with Disabilities Act sets certain employment provisions as law in regard to employing persons with disabilities.

- Seek available community and agency assistance, including potential job mentors and coaches.
- Visit work sites where special-needs persons are employed. Walk through a typical workday, considering each step—getting up in the morning, preparing to go to work, traveling to work, arriving at the workplace, doing various work tasks, eating lunch, relating to other employees, and leaving work.

In Closing

At a board meeting of the Career Development Center of the Southeast, we were reflecting on the image of the church, of all God's created ones, as the body of Christ. One of the board members shared the story of her brother, Bobby, who is challenged with multiple disabilities. She told us how, for her, Bobby exemplifies the way in which God calls and works through individuals, including special-needs people.

At a young age, Bobby was diagnosed with polio. At age nineteen, between his freshman and sophomore years in college, Bobby suffered a serious mental breakdown. He spent half a year in a psychiatric hopsital and was diagnosed with schizophrenia. Because of the polio, he had a distinct limp and had little use of his left hand. Bobby now lives in an efficiency apartment and works full time for an airline catering service.

"When I look at my brother Bobby," she said, "I see the body of Christ. The body is sometimes limping along. Sometimes the body needs medication. Sometimes the body is not in good sync. When I look at Bobby, I see someone I deeply love and someone whom God deeply loves as a member of the body of Christ."

As for everyone, God has a purpose for the special-needs person. The person with disabilities is a part of the body of Christ, and every part is to be valued.

> As it is, there are many members, yet one body. The eye cannot say to the hand, "I have have no need of you," nor again the head to the feet, "I have no need of you." On the contrary, the members of the body that seem to be weaker are indispensable. 1 Corinthians 12:20–22

PART 2

THE CAREER COUNSELING SESSIONS

Introduction to the Sessions

Part 2 contains the six sessions that are fundamental to this career counseling course. Each session begins with background information, called "Thinking It Through," which offers insights on the exercises and may include responses from those who've participated in field testing of this program.

Guidelines for Leaders

It is the leaders' responsibility to make this course more than just a series of self-discovery exercises. This is a faith-based career counseling program, so leaders will need to explain and reinforce the theological concepts, especially those found on page 1 of the journal and described in chapter 4. Reading chapter 2 on God's call and chapter 3 on practices of faith will be helpful as well.

Don't let the term *theological* scare you. Simply put, it means studying God. Everyone does theology, whether they realize it or not. When people think about God or explore their beliefs about God, they are "doing theology." Helping youth and young adults think theologically is what leaders of this course are called to do.

1. Don't Ignore the Spiritual Part of the Program

If you, as a leader, feel uncomfortable discussing spirituality, then approach your work in the program with a willingness to be led by God alongside the participants. You are not alone; we are all learners in the area of spirituality. Remember that the participants are best served when we partner with them in learning.

Don't sell your youth and young adults short by assuming they don't want any "religious" stuff. Don't skip over the Bible studies in each session, assuming that the participants would rather talk about current issues. You'll be surprised at the insights the youth and young adults will share and the connections they will make. Remember, they are searching for God and for meaning in life and want to make these connections. After all, they expect to, at a minimum, talk about God at church.

Be open to the many ways in which the Spirit will work in this group. God has called you as leader. Be open to being transformed by your generous and loving God in this whole career experience. It could be a life-changing experience.

2. Use the Bible in the Sessions

Each session contains a brief study of a Bible passage. Most important, make sure each participant has a Bible. Everyone needs practice using a Bible, so it is better that you use Bibles than copy the relevant passage for each participant. Take the time to engage the participants in a discussion of the passage. Questions for discussion are included for each passage. The additional questions below can be used in the session or any time participants are reading or studying the Bible:

- What came to mind as the passage was read?
- What struck you or occurred to you as you heard it?
- What do you think the writer is trying to say?
- How does the passage speak to us today?
- What do you think God is saying through these words?

3. Be Flexible

Each session is designed to run one and a half hours when used in a group of no more than five participants per leader. If your initial group is larger than five, separate into two groups, each with a leader. This affords time for everyone to share information and experiences. Be flexible. If a particular exercise prompts good discussion and insights, adjust your plan so that you can stay with the discussion. At the same time, don't skip activities. As we mentioned above, leaders could be tempted to omit the Bible studies, assuming the participants prefer the other activities.

If time is running out, save an activity for the next session. Stay late only if the group chooses. Save time for beginning the assignments during the sessions. If the group needs more time, consider having extra sessions. (See chapter 14.)

4. Stress the Importance of Assignments by Starting Them at the End of the Session

The thought of doing homework may cause leaders and participants to skip the assignments. Much of the value of this program will be lost if the participants do not complete the assignments. The best approach is for you to discuss assignments at the first session. Explain the importance of taking time to write in journals, to do some of the practices of faith, and to interview adults. Ask participants for suggestions about how you all can make the career counseling program more meaningful to them. They may decide that they need more than six sessions to complete all the activities, discussions, and assignments prescribed in the six sessions.

5. Be Good Listeners

The essence of this program is listening. A benefit of the program is being a part of a group in which people learn how to talk about themselves. Participants practice articulating their values, beliefs, interests, gifts, and struggles. As people listen to each other, everyone learns, has insights, and makes discoveries. Above all, the group together is on a journey to learn how to listen for God. As a leader, you can model good listening skills.

6. Participate, Especially in the "Question of the Day"

Group members need to get to know their leaders. Therefore, you should participate and share your responses in some of the exercises, as time permits. You should definitely participate in answering the question of the day.

7. Share with the Group the Key Concepts of Career Counseling Ministry

Participants need to know the basic principles and the theological affirmations that are the foundation of this program. In session 1, you will review with them the key concepts of this program. Become familiar with these affirmations so that you can weave them into discussions throughout the sessions. Participants have a copy of the concepts on page 1 of their journals. An explanation of each concept can be found in chapter 4.

Key Concepts of Career Counseling Ministry

1. You are created in God's image. You are a person of infinite worth.
2. God is your partner in exploring, discovering, and living life.
3. You are co-creator with God. God created the world and invites you to continue that creative work, to help make the world what God intended it to be.
4. The key is to stay in conversation with God.
5. You can't make a mistake.
6. The question is not "What do you want to do when you grow up?" Rather, the question is "What do you want to do first?"
7. Career is not just about doing, it's also about being. "What is God calling you to *be* and *do*?"
8. God calls you to a lifestyle, not just a career or occupation.
9. God's call is discovered in community (the we-ness of the call).

The Components of the Career Counseling Ministry Program

Listed below is a summary of the components of the career counseling ministry program. See chapter 4 for a more complete description.

- Six group sessions, occurring weekly or biweekly.
- Additional sessions monthly (or more frequently), for updating one another on current career thinking, plans, mentors, and practices of faith.
- Relationship with one or two adults (preferably two) who lead the group sessions. Two adults are preferred, so that participants can hear two career journey experiences.
- Discussion, plus activities that include filling out self-discovery forms.
- A journal to be kept by each participant.
- Informational interviews—interviews with people about their careers.
- Exploration of the practices of faith.

- Development of a mentor relationship with an adult who may have similar career interests or skills or who may be a role model of faith and lifestyle. (See chapter 6 on mentors.)
- Job site visits—visits with people in careers that interest the participants.
- A parent or guardian session and a parent-participant session. (Descriptions of these sessions are found in chapter 5.)
- A visit to a career counseling center, where participants can take inventories, explore occupations, and talk with a career counselor. The counselor interprets the inventories and sends a report to the participant.
- College trips, sponsored by the church, if possible. If such a trip is not possible, leaders and mentors can keep up with the participants' college searches.

Expectations for the Participants

In the first session, you'll share these hopes and expectations with the participants. We hope:

1. that you'll use this time to:

   - explore God's work in your life (God calls you to a lifestyle of work, faith, family, friends, recreation, service, and relaxation);
   - explore yourself—your gifts, talents, abilities, interests, preferences, and your life past, present, and future;
   - explore the world of work—occupations, skills, and work style;
   - explore practices of faith;
   - explore your creativity—in dreaming and in the activities;

2. that you'll do this exploration "in relationships" (the we-ness of the call), which include leaders, friends, family, significant adult friends, counselors, and mentors;
3. that everyone (leaders and participants) will be open to sharing their journeys, stories, and struggles;
4. that this will be a relaxing time in a time-crunched schedule;
5. that you'll write in your journal. Those who prefer to keep a journal on their computers can find a copy of the journal on the Presbyterian Publishing Corp. Web site. Log on to www.ppcpub.com and click on Download Materials.

Resources and "To Do" List for the Sessions

1. Make copies of the journal pages (twenty-one pages including the journal title page) found in appendix 1, one for each participant. Check the Presbyterian Publishing Corp. Web site, www.ppcpub.com, so that you can refer participants who wish to keep their journal on their computers.
2. Purchase a three-hole-punch folder with pockets for each participant. Assemble the journals with

the pages from appendix 1. Add several blank pages at the back of each.

3. Make copies of the following handouts. They are found at the end of the sessions for which they are needed.

   Life Line Activities (two for each participant) (session 1)

   Life Line Future Highlights (two for each participant) (session 1)

   My Life Line (two for each participant) (session 1) You'll need to create a larger "My Life Line" sheet, using 8 x 14 paper.

   Informational Interview Form (five for each participant) (session 2)

   Skills and Experiences (assigned in session 2 for session 3)

   Discovering Your Gifts (session 3)

   Values and Lifestyle (session 4)

   Risk Taking (session 4)

   Occupations (session 5)

   Occupational Map (session 5)

   Tips for Parents (parent/guardian session, chapter 5)

   Parent Questionnaire (parent-participant session, chapter 5)

   Participant Questionnaire (parent-participant session, chapter 5)

4. Gather resources and materials.

   a journal for each participant
   a file folder for each participant
   Bibles
   pencils and pens
   colored pencils for sessions 1 and 5
   8 x 11 paper for extra journal pages and for sessions 5 and 6
   8 x 11 paper cut in half for session 3
   candle or cross
   clay (session 5)
   your church's hymnal (optional)

5. If there is an interdenominational career center near you, call to see if you can arrange a visit by your group members. Get information about cost, amount of time the testing will take, possible dates for a visit, and registration forms. The center will send you a personal information form for each registrant.

   The visit should take place after the group members have completed the six sessions. You'll need to collect and send the handouts (except the "Informational Interview Form") to the center when you return the completed personal information forms.

6. Collect handouts at the session in which they are completed and keep them in a file folder for each group member.

CHAPTER 8

Session 1—God's Calling: Your Life

Overview

In this first session, you will spend time getting to know one another. As part of the introductions, the adult leaders should share a brief overview of their own career journeys—so far. As in every session, there is a "Question of the Day." With the "Life Line" activities, participants examine their past, present, and projected futures. The Bible study focuses on Ecclesiastes and the concept of time. Participants begin to explore how to "invite God into the conversation." They receive their journals and begin using them in the session.

> God is your partner in exploring, discovering, and living life.

Thinking It Through

In preparation, read chapter 2 on God's call and chapter 3 on the practices of faith. As you plan this session, remember that some of the concepts here will be new to many of the participants. You may find it slow going at first, especially the "Life Line" activities. Assure the participants that this exercise is a way to help them begin thinking about their lives and futures. It also serves as an icebreaker, so encourage participants to talk with one another while they work, perhaps sharing ideas for symbols.

You may find it helpful to lead participants through the "Life Line" exercise using your own life as an example. Write the life activities from the "Life Line Activities" sheet on newsprint or chalkboard. For each, write your age at the time, while asking the participants to guess the age they might be for that activity. For example, for "changing jobs," you might say, "I changed jobs at twenty-nine and again at thirty-two. I'll guess I might change again when I'm forty-two, then again at maybe forty-nine. Take a guess at how many times you'll change jobs and list your age for each." It would be easy to spend the whole session on this exercise. Remember to save time for the Ecclesiastes Bible study and discussions on God's call and inviting God into the conversation.

Thinking about the future can be overwhelming. The future is not just career. It's family life, lifestyle, church, leisure, all activities and interests, in addition to a paid occupation. This will become clear to participants as they pick six highlights of their futures. Most likely, not even half of their highlights will be job related.

Thinking about God's call and inviting God into the conversation may be new concepts for the participants. People vary in their level of faith development and faith expression. One person is perfectly at ease talking about God's presence, while another only occasionally thinks about God. Leaders differ also in their faith expression. If you feel less than comfortable talking

> God calls you to a lifestyle, not just a career/occupation.

about God, you should share this with the participants and express your desire to grow alongside group members as together you and they explore what it means to be in conversation with God. Participants will appreciate your honesty. Moreover, you leaders will be modeling an important part of being a Christian—the idea that Christians are always growing, always learning.

Read chapter 3 on practices of faith for help in explaining practices to the participants.

The book of Ecclesiastes is a natural choice for career exploration. In the introduction to Ecclesiastes, *The New Student Bible* (Grand Rapids: Zondervan Publishing House, 1992) captures the essence of the book with the title "When Life Seems Senseless." Ecclesiastes 3:1–8 is a well-known passage about time. As we field-tested this session, one participant saw a pattern to the phrases indicating balance, order, a cycle of life beginning with birth and ending with peace. Another responded: "There'll be good, there'll be bad; it all happens. But it'll be all right, because God is there and in control. There is balance and meaning to life." Still another picked up on the natural rhythm to life and saw the passage as a reminder, amid the frenetic pace of life, to pay attention to the rhythm of God's created order.

In session 3, participants will look at "who they are." It would be helpful for individuals to take the Myers-Briggs Type Indicator, which identifies people's preferences about numerous activities and from that creates a profile. Many group members may already have taken this test. If your group members are visiting a career center, call the center to see if they will take the test at the center. If this is the case, you can postpone the discussion of the Myers-Briggs until after the center visit.

If participants can take the Myers-Briggs at school or online, or if they know their four-letter type (ESTP, INFJ, for example), you can discuss their results in session 3. Another test, the Keirsey Temperament Sorter II, offers the same four-letter characterization as Myers-Briggs. Both of these instruments are available online: the Myers-Briggs for a fee at www.paladinexec.com; the Keirsey Sorter at www.keirsey.com at no cost. Keirsey can also be found in *Please Understand Me II: Temperament, Character, Intelligence*, by David Keirsey.

At this session, check with group members to see if they can take the test before session 3.

> The key is to stay
> in conversation with God.

Preparation

Make two copies of each for each participant:

"Life Line Activities"
"Life Line Future Highlights" (this can be copied onto the back of "Life Line Activities")
"My Life Line" (On an 8 x 14 sheet, draw a line lengthwise that divides the paper in half, so that there are four inches above and below the line. Copy the age marks from page 74.)

Copy the twenty-one journal pages (including journal title page) from appendix 1 for each participant. Add several blank pages at the back of the journal. You'll need:

handouts
a journal for each participant
a file folder for each participant
Bibles
pencils
colored pencils (three colors for each person)
candle or cross
hymnals (optional)

The Session

1. Inviting God into the Conversation

Open with prayer. Make sure that people know each other. Use a simple introduction activity such as "Say your name, favorite movie, and a good thing that happened to you this week."

2. Question of the Day

Ask: "When you were a little kid, what was one of the things you wanted to be when you grew up?" Everyone is invited to answer, including the leaders.

3. Vocational Journeys

Leaders share their own vocational journeys. (Avoid lecturing or preaching about how it "should" be. Simply share how your journey has gone—up to now.)

4. Key Concepts, Expectations, and Process

Distribute the journals. Spend a few minutes talking about the key concepts of career counseling ministry (which can be found on the first page of the journal, "Take Note: This Is Important"), the process, the expectations (see "Introduction to the Sessions," page 63), and resolving basic issues:

- Decide on a regular day and time to meet for future sessions.
- If you have planned a career center visit after the six sessions or are planning a college trip, discuss the details. If the group is going to a career center for testing, all of the handouts (activity sheets) should be sent to the center prior to the visit. Centers appreciate having as much information from their clients as possible. Whether or not there is a center visit, you will collect the activity sheets at the end of the sessions in which they are completed and keep them in individual file folders.
- Explain the program. The six sessions cover three topics: "God's Calling," "About You," and "The World of Work." In this first session we'll look at how you can invite God into the conversation about career, lifestyle, vocation, and so forth. You'll look at your life, past and present, and identify where God has been present. And we'll explore together what it means that God calls.
- Discuss the idea and importance of assignments and journal writing and that time will be given during each session to begin that week's assignment.
- Remind everyone to bring their journals and Bibles to each meeting. If participants want to keep the journals on their computers, they can access the Presbyterian Publishing Corp. Web site at www.ppcpub.com.
- Ask who has taken the Myers-Briggs. If participants can arrange to take the Myers-Briggs or the Keirsey Temperament Sorter II, ask them to take it before session 3, as they will discuss their four-letter type at that session. If there is a center visit, call to see if the center administers the Myers-Briggs.

> God's call is discovered in community (the we-ness of the call). Therefore, career counseling is best done "in relationship," emphasizing the importance of the group, friends, family, and significant adult friends in the church.

5. My Life Line—Past, Present, and Future

In this exercise, participants look at where they have been, where they are, and where they are going. They note significant events, activities, and accomplishments from their past and the present, identifying those at which they were particularly aware of God's presence. Then they will think about the future, about events that they think may occur.

Distribute two copies of each of the following (one copy for participants and one for them to take home to parents/guardians):

> "Life Line Activities"
> "Life Line Future Highlights"
> "My Life Line"

LIFE LINE ACTIVITIES
The participants complete this sheet first, following the instructions. This exercise invites creativity, as group members create symbols for each activity. This part of the exercise takes time, so encourage people to help one another devise symbols to avoid frustration.

LIFE LINE FUTURE HIGHLIGHTS
On this sheet, participants draw pictures or symbols to represent six events that they expect will be important highlights in their future.

MY LIFE LINE
On the "My Life Line" sheet, which is a time line with age markings along the line, participants should:

1. transfer symbols from the "Life Line Activities" sheet to their life line;
2. transfer symbols from the "Future Highlights" sheet to their life line;
3. identify significant events, activities, or accomplishments in their past by putting them in the appropriate place on their life line, using one or two words;
4. next, look at the events they've written, and identify where God was present in specific events and activities; they are to mark these with a cross;

5. last, with different colored pencils (not markers), indicate by underlining or shading on their life lines those years in which they expect to be

- working (one color)
- married (a second color)
- with children at home (a third color)

Assure everyone that you do not presume everyone will marry and have children. The purpose is to offer perspective on life span and lifestyle. For instance, they will discover that they are likely to have a lot of years beyond "children at home" or "working," especially if they consider a retirement age of sixty-five.

Discuss the life lines by asking:

- What did you learn about yourself and your life?
- From the highlights you chose, what are you discovering about your values, about what's important to you?

6. Sharing with Parents or Guardians

Suggest that participants take an extra copy of "My Life Line," "Life Line Activities," and "Life Line Future Highlights" for a parent, stepparent, grandparent, or guardian to complete. This is a good way to encourage parents or guardians and their youth or young adult sons and daughters to talk about life, about dreams, and about God's presence as they share their life lines with one another.

Discuss with participants the possibilities of parents taking on the role of partner during the career counseling process. Such a partnership can take the parent-child relationship to a new level and counter the natural move for youth and young adults to distance themselves from their parents. Young adults, especially, have a fear of being seen as a failure by their parents.

Ask the group:

- Do you worry about being seen as a failure in your parents' eyes?
- In what ways might the partner concept improve relationships between you and your parents?

7. Insight from Scripture

Ecclesiastes 3:1-8

Everything has a time—and a season—and a reason. Suggest that participants follow along in their Bibles as a leader reads Ecclesiastes 3:1–8.

Ask:
- What came to mind as I read this passage?
- What do you think about the concept of time? Does it seem to creep along or fly by? Do you feel as if you never have enough time, or do you think you have too much time on your hands?
- Is time managing you, or are you managing time?
- Going back to your earliest memories as a child, what were the significant events in your life? Was God or church a part of any of them?
- Projecting forward into the future, if you could dream of a life you would like to live, what would it include? How would God be a part of this dream? How would church be a part?

8. The Journal

Participants should keep a journal of their reflections and discoveries on their career journey. Invite everyone to turn to page 4. Encourage participants to write on this page in their journals during the discussion.

CALLED BY GOD
The first question on page 4 is: What does it mean to be called by God?
Ask:

- What do you think it means that God calls us?
- Instead of thinking about what God calls us to do, let's think about what God calls us to be and to do. God called us into being. God breathed life into us. What do you think God is calling you and me and others to be?
- What do you think God is calling us to do? There is no one answer. This morning God may be calling you to reach out to someone. Later in the day God may be calling you to rest. Tonight God may be calling you to share your journey with someone.
- How does God call us? How does God call you?

INVITING GOD INTO THE CONVERSATION AND PRACTICES OF FAITH
Prayer is one of the ways by which we discover what God is calling us to be and do. But what is prayer? How do we pray? Prayer takes many forms. It is more than bowing heads and "sending up requests and thank-yous." Prayer is talking with God. Prayer is listening for God. Prayer is inviting God into the conversations we have with one another about our lives, our careers, and about decisions we have to make. Prayer can be writing, singing, meditating, dancing.

Prayer is one of the practices of faith that help us listen for God, learn more about God, grow closer to Jesus Christ, and discover God's will. Throughout the career counseling process, we'll be exploring various practices. The second half of page 4 in your journal offers space for listing practices of faith or ways to listen for God.

Ask:

- What are some other practices of faith?
- How can they help you?
- Which practices are already a part of your life?
- Which would you like to add to your life?

Have everyone look at pages 5 and 6 in their journals, "Practices of Faith." Invite them to select a practice to begin practicing, such as prayer, meditation, Bible study, sabbath time, or journal writing.

Discuss ways to help one another. Leader: Share information from chapter 3 on the practices of faith.

9. Assignment

In the journal, on page 2, "Dreaming about the Future," participants are to list things, anything they hope will be a part of their life in the future. Take a few minutes and do that now. If participants begin using the journal during the group session, they are more likely to use it at home. Remind them to bring journals to the next session.

Encourage everyone to give parents or guardians the "Life Line" exercise. They will have a chance to talk about the experience of sharing with parents at the next session.

If participants have completed the "Life Line" sheets, collect them and put them in their folders. They can take them home to share with parents, provided they bring them back.

10. Closing

Now and whenever during a session you invite God into the conversation, consider placing a cross or lighted candle in the center of the group to help people focus on God's presence. A candle serves as a reminder of God's light among us and in the world. Both candle and cross remind us of Christ's presence with us.

> Career is not just about doing, it's also about being. What is God calling you to *be* and *do*?

Close with prayer. Consider including the lyrics from a hymn related to God's call. Check your church's hymnal. Possible hymns include:

"Be Thou My Vision"
"Here I Am, Lord"
"I'm Gonna Live So God Can Use Me"
"Called as Partners in Christ's Service"
"Come, Labor On"
"God, Whose Giving Knows No Ending"
"Lord, You Give the Great Commission"
"Canto de Esperanza" (Song of Hope)
"Arise, Your Light is Come!"
"Breathe on Me, Breath of God"
"What Does the Lord Require"
"Take My Life"

Name _____

Life Line Activities*

1. For each item below, write the age the event occurred in your life, or for those events that may happen in the future, the age when you estimate it may occur.

2. Then think up a symbol to represent each activity and draw this symbol next to your age.

Activity	Your estimated age for each	Symbol
Childhood	_____	_____
Begin high school	_____	_____
Graduate from high school	_____	_____
Further education	_____	_____
Military experience	_____	_____
First job	_____	_____
Marriage	_____	_____
First child born	_____	_____
Raising children, changing jobs	_____	_____
Last child born	_____	_____
Settling into an occupation	_____	_____
Several job changes	_____	_____
Last child enters school	_____	_____
Occupational peak	_____	_____
Children leave home	_____	_____
Grandchildren born	_____	_____
Retirement	_____	_____
Travel, leisure	_____	_____

* Adapted from "Spiritmasters" for David P. Campbell's *If You Don't Know Where You're Going, You'll Probably End Up Somewhere Else* (Allen, Tex.: RCL Enterprises Inc., 1974).

Life Line Future Highlights

In the circles below, draw pictures or symbols to represent six events that you expect to be important highlights in your life.

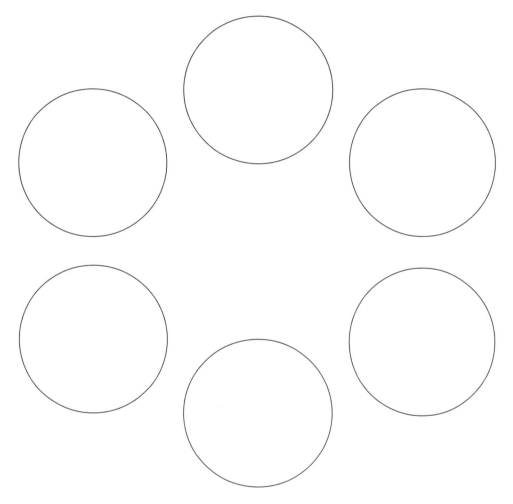

Using the "My Life Line" sheet:

1. transfer the symbols from the "Life Line Activities" sheet onto the life line;

2. transfer the symbols from the "Future Highlights" sheet onto the life line;

3. identify significant events, activities, or accomplishments in your past, and place them on the life line, using one or two words;

4. identify those events at which you were particularly aware of God's presence, and mark them with a cross;

5. with a colored pencil, underline or shade those years on the life line you expect to be:

- working (one color)
- married (a second color)
- with children at home (a third color)

Name _____

My Life Line

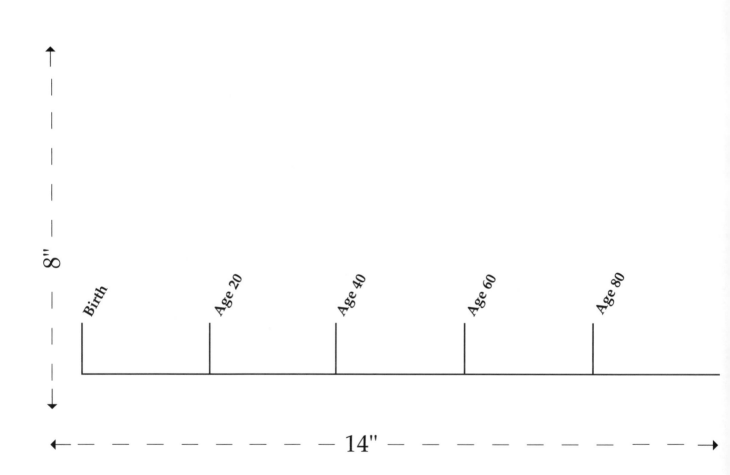

CHAPTER 9

Session 2—God's Calling: Your Dream

Overview

In this session, participants dream about the future through a guided fantasy exercise. They consider what they value in life as they think about what their lives may look like in the future. In the Genesis Bible study, participants look at the role God plays in their lives and the roles God may be calling them to play in life.

Thinking It Through

This session begins where session 1 left off, with the two assignments—the sharing of the "Life Line" experience with parents or guardians and journal writing. Participants may find completing assignments difficult, especially if they are in school. Assure them of the importance of making time for reflection. Taking the time to share discoveries from assignments and hearing others' discoveries will help everyone see the value of the assignments.

The fantasy future exercise uses a technique known as guided imagery, which will be new to many people. Even though some people feel awkward closing their eyes and getting into the exercise, many participants later cite this as their favorite exercise in the program.

The discussion will be enlightening. One girl, whose dream was to live in New York City and work backstage in theater, was disappointed after the exer-

cise, for she discovered that she was very lonely living this dream. We cautioned her not to overreact and give up her dream but to be aware of the challenges that any vocation brings. Loneliness accompanies many careers, especially when a move is involved. Participating in career counseling ministry prepares people for life and vocation, for it gives them the opportunity to identify and explore with one another ways of dealing with a variety of factors.

With this session, the group should begin to think of creative ways to close their time together in prayer or with another practice of faith. Participating in decision making increases their ownership in the group and enables the "bonding" that so many youth and young adults talk about when they speak of their best group experiences.

> You are a co-creator with God.
> God created the world and invites you to continue that creative work, to help make the world what God intended it to be.

Preparation

Make five copies for each participant:

"Informational Interview Form"

Make one copy for each participant:

"Skills and Experiences"

You'll need:

handouts
journals

file folders
Bibles
pencils
candle or cross

The Session

1. Inviting God into the Conversation

Open with prayer. Have participants share insights they gained from having their parents or guardians do the "My Life Line" exercise.

2. Question of the Day

Complete this sentence: "I can't imagine life without . . . " Everyone should answer, including leaders. Invite everyone to write answers in their journals on page 3.

3. Dreams about the Future

For their assignment from session 1, participants worked on page 2 in the journals, listing things they hoped would be a part of their lives in the future. Invite everyone to share their comments.
Ask:

- What did you learn about yourself doing this activity?
- What surprised you?

4. Fantasy Future

This exercise uses a technique known as guided imagery. Its purpose is to give people a chance to relax and envision a future scene. The leader must read the exercise slowly, pausing after each question, so that participants have time to envision details.

Begin by telling everyone that they will be doing a guided imagery exercise. Acknowledge that it may seem strange to them at first, but they should try it and see what happens. Tell them they will be closing their eyes and envisioning their life ten years from now. Next, tell them to get comfortable, wherever they wish—in their chairs, on the floor, and so forth.

THE EXERCISE
Close your eyes, relax, shut out the outside world. Take a deep breath. Exhale. Relax your neck, your shoulders, your arms. Let all the tension out of your body. Breathe in. Breathe out. Listen to yourself breathing. Breathe in. Breathe out. Let your mind create images as I ask each question.

Picture yourself ten years from now. How old are you? Where are you? Where do you live—the city? a town? on a farm? What kind of a residence do you have—house? apartment? Where is it? What does it look like outside, what's around your place? Who lives with you? family?

It's Monday morning. Your alarm goes off. What time is it? Notice what your room looks like. Are you alone? You get up and get dressed for work. What are you wearing? You are excited about going to work, for this is your vocation, the job you had always hoped to have. You love your work.

You have breakfast. Where are you eating? What are you eating? Who prepared it? Who is with you? You feel wonderful. Notice how good you feel about yourself. God is happy with you.

It's time to go to work. Do you stay at home or go somewhere? What are you taking with you to work? briefcase? bag? laptop? lunch? extra clothes? Where are you going? How do you get there—walk? drive? take public transportation? train, bus, what? How do things look along the way? Do you see people you know?

You arrive at work. What time is it? Where are you? In what kind of place do you work? Are you indoors? outdoors? Picture the route you take to get to your actual workplace where you start your workday. Who's there? Think of adjectives to describe what you look like at this place (longer pause here).

Experience this vocation. What does your day look like? Are you sitting, walking around, changing locations, traveling, on the phone? Are you by yourself? with colleagues? Are you the boss—of some? of everyone? Do you have a boss? What type of person is your boss? Describe the people you work with. What are they doing? Do you have a title? What is it?

What kinds of activities are you doing—filing, digging, working with papers, writing, teaching, seeing clients, in meetings, operating machines, checking things, working at a computer, talking on the phone? What?

It's lunchtime. Do you stay in or go out? If out, where do you go and how do you get there? What are you eating? Are you alone or with others? Who—friends? business associates? clients? kids? How long do you have for lunch?

Return to work. Remember, you still are having a *great* day! You know that this is the vocation you are called to do. What's different about the afternoon? What time do you finish the day's work?

Where do you go after work? Do you take work home with you? How—in a briefcase, laptop, or other bag? What work do you take home? When will you do this work?

What activities do you have planned for the evening? with whom? What time do you go to bed?

What are you looking forward to this week? this month? Think about volunteer activities, church, recreation, family time, relaxation (longer pause here).

You have just had a wonderful day! Have a good night's sleep! Take a deep breath, exhale. Slowly come back to the group.

Invite participants to talk about the experience. Ask:

- What did you discover about yourself? Any surprises?
- What did you like about your fantasy?
- What didn't you like?
- Where did you live?
- What was your career?
- How did you feel about it?

If some had a hard time with images or answers, or if they drifted off, affirm them; it's okay. They'll benefit from listening to others.

"Lord, you have been our dwelling place in all generations.
Before the mountains were brought forth, or ever you had formed the earth and the world,
from everlasting to everlasting you are God."

Psalm 90:1–2

5. Insight from Scripture

Genesis 1—The Creation Story;
Genesis 12:2—Blessed to Be a Blessing

Part of inviting God into our conversation is discovering the role God plays in our lives. From the very beginning, God created and blessed us and called us to care for God's creation.

1. Invite participants to review the first twenty-five verses of Genesis 1 in their Bibles and to recall what God created.
2. Have someone in the group read Genesis 1:26–31 aloud.
3. Ask:

   - What's special about human beings?
   - What role does God give human beings?
   - What does that role suggest to you in terms of thinking about a career? Does the passage suggest that farmer and environmentalist are the only career possibilities?

- In what ways can people care for God's creation?
- If God created this world and supplies us with everything, then do we need to put forth any effort of our own?
- If you think everything is not supplied for you, what role does God play in your life?

4. Have another member read Genesis 12:2 aloud. This verse may shed light on the previous questions. God has blessed us so that we may be a blessing to others.
5. Ask:

   - In what ways can people be a blessing to others in their vocations?
   - How might this verse become a theme for your lifestyle? In other words, how might you live out the theme that you are "blessed to be a blessing"?
   - How does this relate to what God may be calling us to be and do?

6. Inviting God into the Conversation

Allow time for relaxed sharing and discussion of the practices of faith that individuals are beginning to try. Invite the group members to share discoveries they make as they endeavor to listen for God. Discuss the difficulties they may be encountering with the practices.

Decide together on a particular form of prayer with which to close the session, perhaps praying a psalm. If you do select a psalm, such as Psalm 103:1–13, have one person read the verses. After each odd-numbered verse, the group will say, "We thank you, generous God." Suggest that as people continue their practices during the week, they think of creative ways to close each session.

7. Assignment

Before closing the session, distribute the "Skills and Experiences" sheet that will be discussed in session 3. Review the instructions with the group:

1. Think of eight activities that you have particularly enjoyed in the past four years. (Activities could include full-time or part-time jobs, tasks, projects, achievements,

volunteer activities, hobbies, leadership opportunities, family responsibilities, helping a friend with a problem, and school events, such as performances, sports, awards you have been given.) You may think of an activity you did not initially expect to enjoy. List the activities on p. 79, one after each number.

2. In the space beneath each activity, list the skills you used to accomplish the activity.

3. After each skill, put a D, P, I, or T (representing Data, People, Ideas, or Things) to indicate the category to which you would assign that particular skill. Some skills may involve more than one category.

> God's call is discovered in community (the we-ness of the call). Friends, family, mentors, and significant adult friends in the church all play a role.

Data: working with information, numbers, records—computing
People: working with people, face-to-face—teaching, counseling, helping, selling, persuading
Ideas: working with ideas—creating, envisioning, brainstorming, studying, writing
Things: working with your hands—building, repairing, operating

Example: Planning the Science Fair

Sharing ideas   I
Visioning   I
Writing a plan and schedule   D
Designing a floor plan   I, D
Attending to details   D, P
Phoning   P
Leading meetings   P
Encouraging others' involvement   P
Listening   P
Organizing materials   D, T
Building booths   T

Allow a few minutes for the group to begin work on this sheet. They should bring the completed form to the next session.

Collect the "Life Line" activity sheets and put them in the group members' file folders.

INFORMATIONAL INTERVIEWS (AN ASSIGNMENT OVER TIME)

Also distribute five "Informational Interview Forms" to each participant. Explain that each member is to contact at least three people who have jobs that interest them or jobs requiring skills they are discovering they have or would like to have. Or they can choose a person whom they admire. They are to complete an "Informational Interview Form" for each interview.

This exercise gives participants interview experience (even though they are the interviewers). They also learn how to make contacts, which is part of networking. And networking is a valuable tool for discovering careers or jobs that may be a part of what God is calling them to be and do. The leader should remind people of the importance of getting these interviews.

MENTORS

Suggest that the interviews may help participants find mentors. Remind them of the role a mentor plays: mentors are people who care enough about youth and young adults to become significant adult friends. They are good listeners who can share in the struggles and decisions of career search and faith journey. They can arrange job site visits for the participants and introduce them to others who can share stories of discerning call.

Participants who identify a potential mentor can either begin to develop that relationship themselves or tell a career counseling leader, who can make the contact. People are flattered to be asked to be mentors, but they must be accurately informed of their responsibilities. See chapter 6 for more information on mentors.

If your church has a mentor program, encourage the participants to look for mentors through that program. And encourage your group members to be observers of people—to notice people's vocations, lifestyles, the manner in which they live out their faith and express their values.

8. Closing

Close in whatever way the group has decided.

Name _____

Skills and Experiences

1. Think of eight activities that you have particularly enjoyed in the past four years. (Activities could include full-time or part-time jobs, tasks, projects, achievements, volunteer activities, hobbies, leadership opportunities, family responsibilities, helping a friend with a problem, and school events, such as performances, sports, awards you have been given.) You may think of an activity you did not initially expect to enjoy. List the activities below, one after each number (use back of your sheet if necessary).
2. In the space beneath each activity, list the skills you used to accomplish the activity.
3. After each skill, put a D, P, I, or T (representing Data, People, Ideas, or Things) to indicate the category to which you would assign that particular skill. Some skills may involve more than one category.

Data:	working with information, numbers, records—computing
People:	working with people, face-to-face—teaching, counseling, helping, selling, persuading
Ideas:	working with ideas—creating, envisioning, brainstorming, studying, writing
Things:	working with your hands—building, repairing, operating

Example: Planning the Science Fair

Sharing ideas   I
Visioning   I
Writing a plan and schedule   D
Designing a floor plan   I, D
Attending to details   D, P
Phoning   P
Leading meetings   P
Encouraging others' involvement   P
Listening   P
Organizing materials   D, T
Building booths   T

1)

2)

3)

4)

5)

6)

7)

8)

Name _____

Informational Interview Form

1. Phone people you'd like to interview and ask if you can talk with them about their work. Ask for the interview by saying: "To find out about different jobs, a career counseling group in my church is interviewing several people about their work. I am interested in (the person's work) and would like to ask you a few questions." Tell them that the interview will take only fifteen to twenty minutes.
2. Don't be shy about asking for an interview. Almost everyone likes to talk about their work.
3. Use the questions below in interviewing people about their work. Feel free to add your own questions to this list.

Name of interviewee _____ Occupation _____

1. For whom do you work? _____

2. What do you do? _____

3. How did you choose this occupation? _____
_____

4. How old were you when you decided on this vocation? _____

5. What other careers have you seriously considered? _____
_____

6. Why do you enjoy your work? _____
_____

7. Is there a lot of variety in your daily tasks? _____

8. What activities on your job do you enjoy most? _____
_____

9. What activities do you enjoy least? _____

10. Can you tell me about a time when a particularly good thing happened to you at work? _____
_____

11. Can you tell about a bad time at work? _____
_____

12. Do you expect to be in this job ten years from now? What else might you be doing? _____
_____

13. Are there opportunities for young people in your field? _____
_____

14. What kind of people tend to do well in your job? _____
_____

15. What kind of people do you work with? Do you like them? _____
_____

16. What's the typical salary in your field? _____

17. What is the best education or training for the work you do? _____
_____

CHAPTER 10

Session 3—About You: Skills, Gifts, and Interests

Overview

Sessions 3 and 4 contain exercises that help participants identify their skills, gifts, and interests. The group will begin work on the "Assets" section of their journals. Assets are a person's positives, the things a person has going for her or him. The more assets a person can identify, the easier it should be to pursue a vocation that fits the person's interests, gifts, and preferences, because developing assets is an important part of the career journey.

The passage from 1 Corinthians expresses the importance and necessity of having a variety of gifts in order for the body of Christ to be what God created it to be.

Thinking It Through

Good career counseling is more about helping individuals know themselves than it is about looking at vocations. To find a fulfilling career and lifestyle, people should spend more time answering the question "Who am I?" than "What career should I pursue?"

Therefore, participants will spend a lot of time in sessions 3 and 4 talking about themselves. Some people are better at this than others. Everybody should learn how to talk about their gifts and talents without being embarrassed or worrying about sounding egotistical. Interviews, for both jobs and schools, require that people be able to present themselves well, to talk about what they can offer the school or company. Talking about interests is good practice, especially for those who aren't sure what really interests them. The group can serve as a sounding board and can ask questions for clarification. The members can help one another learn the skills of selling themselves. Recognizing that they are created in the image of God and loved by God will be a confidence booster.

As part of the discussion on "Interests," you will ask the participants to combine two of their interests and create a job out of the two. They should enjoy this activity, for some of the outcomes will be a little ridiculous. Point out that this exercise fosters creativity, and a creative mind is highly valued in today's world of work. In fact, combining your interests is an excellent way to discover what God may be calling you to do at some point in your life.

The "Skills and Experiences" exercise helps participants discover the skills they enjoy using and identify the areas in which their skills lie by using four categories: People, Data, Ideas, Things. People usually find they are more comfortable working in one or two of those areas. By listing activities and achievements they've enjoyed, the participants should be able to identify skills they enjoy using.

In addition to identifying the skills they both enjoy and do well, participants should identify the skills they want to develop. My job requires me to do public speaking, which I don't always enjoy because I feel quite inadequate; but it's at the top of my list of skills I want to develop. Leaders, choose an example from your life so that participants will see that developing skills is a lifelong effort.

Another reason for identifying skills is to develop an understanding of transferable skills. In a culture where people change jobs and careers frequently, it's crucial to identify how skills used in one job can be used in, or transferred to, the next job.

A friend of mine who was an excellent middle

school counselor considered applying for the position of principal at her school. At first she was overwhelmed by the thought of being an administrator, but when she examined her skills—listening, counseling, conflict managing, serving (people skills), and synthesizing information (data skills), she saw that these were transferable skills that would also make her a good principal. She believed she would enjoy developing the administrative skills the job required, so she applied and received the job. It's those transferable skills (from her counseling job) that have made her one of our finest principals, because she truly cares about the middle schoolers, and they know it.

This session's scripture passage, 1 Corinthians 12, stresses the absolute necessity and importance of all gifts to the body of Christ, the community of faith: "There are different kinds of gifts, but the same Spirit. There are different kinds of service, but the same Lord. There are different kinds of working, but the same God works all of them in all [people]" (vv. 4–6 NIV). It is reassuring for people to know that, in God's order, "the members of the body that seem to be weaker are indispensable," (v. 22 NRSV). "But God has so arranged the body, giving the greater honor to the inferior member" (v. 24b NRSV).

The "Discovering Your Gifts" exercise is based on 1 Corinthians 12:7, "To each is given the manifestation of the Spirit for the common good," and reminds us that our gifts are not to be used selfishly. We are called to use them for others. Filling out the "Gifts" sheet is a confidence builder, for the participants explore the gifts God has given them. They may be surprised by characteristics that they had never before considered gifts, let alone gifts from God.

Preparation

Make one copy for each participant:

> "Skills and Experiences" (located at the end of session 2) Make extra copies in case participants didn't bring their copies, which were distributed at the last session.
> "Discovering Your Gifts"

Make extra copies of the "Informational Interview Form" which was distributed at the previous session. Group members may need additional forms.
You'll need:

> handouts
> journals
> file folders

Bibles
pencils
half sheet of paper for each person for the closing
candle or cross

The Session

1. Inviting God into the Conversation

Ask the participants to share their experiences trying a practice of faith. What have they been doing? Using a prayer of your choice, invite God into the conversations that will be a part of this session.

2. Question of the Day

"What adjectives would you use to describe yourself?" Invite participants to list these on page 3 of their journals. Everyone can share some or all of their list.

3. Skills and Experiences

As part of the homework assignment from session 2, participants should have filled out the "Skills and Experiences" sheet, which suggests that skills can be grouped into four categories: Data, People, Ideas, Things. The idea here is for people to identify skills that they particularly enjoy using. If participants have not finished the sheet, they should do that now. The instructions are both on the handout on p. 79 and in session 2 on p. 77.

Invite participants to review their completed sheets. Ask:

- Looking at all your activities, what skills are repeated?
- Which skills do you consider yourself "good at"?
- Count the Ds, Ps, Is, and Ts. In which category do you have the most? second most? least?
- What did you learn about yourself from this exercise?
- Which skills would you like to develop?

Talk about transferable skills, that skills used in one career or job can be used in another (see "Thinking It Through" above). Discuss ways in which the skills listed on the sheet can be transferable.

4. Personality Type

If the group members have taken the Myers-Briggs Type Indicator or the Keirsey Temperament Sorter II, discuss the results. Invite participants to share their four-letter types and what they discovered about themselves from the test. Postpone this activity if participants are visiting a career center after completing the six sessions. Most likely they will take the Myers-Briggs there and have it interpreted by a counselor. They will enjoy sharing results at an additional session.

5. Insight from Scripture

1 Corinthians 12:4–6; 12–20; 21–27

1. Ask everyone to turn in their Bibles to 1 Corinthians 12 and to read verses 4, 5, and 6. The verses make three statements about things that are different and things that are the same.
2. Ask:

   * From this passage, what three things are meant to be different?
   * What do these verses say is the same?

3. Invite someone to read verses 12–27.
4. Ask:

   * What do these verses tell you about the body of Christ, the church?
   * What do they tell you about your role in the body of Christ? about your role in the world?
   * In what way have you have felt inferior or weaker, that your abilities were not as important as someone else's?
   * What does this passage tell you about vocation?

6. Discovering Your Gifts

1. Distribute the "Discovering Your Gifts" sheet. This exercise builds self-esteem, as people are usually impressed with the number of items they can check on this list of gifts.
2. Ask participants to mark all the characteristics/ gifts that apply to them. When they have completed the form, discuss the following questions:

   * What did you learn about yourself?
   * Which of the gifts would you like to develop?

3. Read 1 Corinthians 12:7.

4. Ask:

   * According to this passage, how are we supposed to use our gifts?
   * What does "for the common good" mean?

7. Assets

Explain that assets are the things you have going for you—skills, education, experiences, motivation— those things that might cause an employer to choose you over another candidate. The more assets you can identify, the easier it should be to pursue a vocation that fits your interests, gifts, and preferences. It is important to develop and accumulate assets, for the more you have, the more choices you will have for your future.

Begin by introducing and discussing the nine assets in the journals (pages 7–15). They are: (1) skills, gifts, talents, and abilities; (2) motivation; (3) friends; (4) education; (5) lifelong learning; (6) family; (7) experiences; (8) faith experiences; and (9) personal characteristics and health. Tell participants to begin writing on these pages during the discussion. Emphasize the importance of journaling, and remind them to date their entries.

8. Interests

Identifying interests is a primary requirement for being able to follow your dream and find a career and lifestyle that fulfill who you are and what God is calling you to be and do.

1. Have participants turn to the "Interests" page (page 16) in their journals. Invite them to list a few answers to each question. Suggest that they look back on this page in the next few years to see how their interests have changed. Have the participants share answers. The following is a list of the questions from the "Interests" page:

   * Quickly list everything you can think of that interests you. What do you just love to do?
   * When you walk into a bookstore, which section do you go to first? What other sections do you visit?
   * Imagine that you are going to a mall that has every possible kind of store that exists. In which stores would you enjoy spending time browsing?

> Career is not just about doing, it's also about being. What is God calling you to be and do?

- When you pick up a newspaper, which sections do you read? Why?
- What do you enjoy talking about? If you were stuck on a plane for eight hours and the person next to you wanted to talk, what subjects or fields would make the time fly by?
- When you browse the Web, what topics do you like to enter?
- Someone has offered to pay you to go anywhere in the world to study for three weeks at any university/school/training program. Where would you go? What would you study?

Ask:

- What does this tell you about yourself?

2. Have group members look at their list of interests, the things they love to do. Tell them to take the first and third items and create a job combining the two interests. Participants should come up with some crazy ideas. Invite them to share their innovations. This is an exercise in creativity, a highly valued quality in today's world of work. If time permits, have them combine two other interests and create another occupation.

9. Assignment

1. Continue working on the "Assets" section of the journal (pages 7–15).

2. Begin getting informational interviews. "Informational Interview Forms" were distributed at the last session. Additional forms are available.

3. Keep an eye out for mentors. Someone out there would love to be your mentor, to help you think through decisions, to share insights and challenges about life and work.

10. Closing

Ask if anyone has a suggestion for this session's closing. Consider incorporating the "Gifts" list as part of the practice of offering. Ask participants what comes to mind when they think of offering as a practice of faith (stewardship, worship, money, giving of self).

Invite participants to choose one or two gifts from those they checked on their "Discovering Your Gifts" sheet that they would like to offer to God. They can write these on a half sheet of paper. In a prayer of dedication, they can ask God to use the gifts in service to God and others. Participants can place the slips of paper at the foot of a cross or candle that has been placed in the center of the group.

Collect the completed "Skills and Experiences" sheets and the "Discovering Your Gifts" sheets. Put them in the group members' file folders.

Name _____

Discovering your Gifts*

"To each is given the manifestation of the Spirit for the common good." (1 Corinthians 12:7 NRSV)

Check the gifts listed below that you feel you have been given by God.

___Intelligence

___Athletic ability

___Musical talent

___Acting talent

___Sensitivity

___Compassion

___Integrity

___Imagination

___Enthusiasm

___Manual skills

___Verbal skills

___Listening skills

___Mechanical skills

___Sense of caution

___Creativity

___Commitment

___Spontaneity

___Patience

___An easy going nature

___Problem-solving skills

___Willingness to work hard

___Other _____

___Other _____

___Sense of justice

___Detail-oriented

___Ability to teach

___Leadership skills

___Peacemaking skills

___Artistic ability

___Loyalty

___Approachability

___Organizational skills

___Efficiency

___Ability to encourage

___Ability to delegate

___Motivation

___Ability to support friends

___Willingness to take risks

___Realistic outlook on life

___Skills for interacting with children

___Skills for interacting with older people

___Willingness to do thankless jobs

___Other _____

___Other _____

___Humor

___Cooking skills

___Practicality

___Ability to plan

___Dependability

___Friendliness

___Gentleness

___Love

___Kindness

___Generosity

___Courage

___Honesty

___Affection

___Vision

___Strength

___Empathy

*Adapted from Paul M. Thompson and Joani Lillevold Schultz, *The Giving Book: A Creative Resource for Senior High Ministry* (Atlanta: John Knox Press, 1985), 83.

CHAPTER 11

Session 4—About You: Values, Lifestyle, and Risk

Overview

In this session, participants continue to discover more about themselves. They examine their values, what's important to them in life. Identifying interests, done in session 3, and claiming values are critical steps we all must take to help determine the kinds of life we want. When interests are linked to a desire to respond to God's call, people can make better career decisions. There can, however, be a huge gap between having self-knowledge and doing something about it. This session looks at risk taking and family, two critical factors that can stop a person from venturing out and getting on with the journey. The good news is that both can be positive factors as well.

Thinking It Through

A key concept of this program is that God calls us to both a lifestyle and a vocation. To think only about a career, how to make a living, is like looking at a rainbow and seeing only one color. The enjoyment is in seeing the multiple colors. Only then is the rainbow a magnificent natural work of art. God calls us to a lifestyle and a vocation in which career is only one color in the rainbow. To focus narrowly on a career is to miss out on the glorious life God intends.

In session 3, participants identified interests and gifts that related to areas of life besides career. God's good gifts are to be used in every area of life. As the group members become comfortable with practices of faith and inviting God into the conversation, they will make connections between faith and work and between faith and lifestyle.

An important factor in thinking about vocation, lifestyle, and decision making is the risk factor. In making decisions, we weigh the consequences of a choice; we count the cost and then decide whether we are willing to take the risk. I grew up in a family where safety was always the primary concern, so I've labeled myself as a non–risk taker. To divide the population into risk takers and non–risk takers, however, is an oversimplification.

Sean Covey, in *The Seven Habits of Highly Effective Teens,* defines being in the comfort zone as staying within the confines of things, places, and activities that are familiar and nonthreatening. There we feel safe, secure, and risk free, but we are never stretched, and as a result, our learning and our experience are limited. Covey calls the area beyond your comfort zone your "courage zone." In a courage zone, you try things you've never tried or that you're afraid of—difficult things, challenges, adventures. These things include opportunity, higher duty, bravery, and ultimate potential.[1]

In the movie *A League of Their Own,* which is about the first women's baseball league, one of the players wants to quit and go home. She cries to her coach, "It's just too hard." The coach replies, "Of course, it's hard, but being hard is what makes it great."

Healthy risk taking is a quality to be desired, and participants will examine here their willingness to take four kinds of risk: physical risks, financial risks, interpersonal risks, and intellectual risks. These categories are helpful, for they help us see the truth about our actions. For example, we don't often think of something like a reluctance to call someone on the phone as having anything to do with risk taking, yet it involves interpersonal risk. Participants will find they are likely to be more willing to take risks in some areas than in others.

We invite participants to look at the role families play—the positive and negative messages we get from our families. Identifying the negative messages can help us recognize the negative feelings they leave with us. Understanding how the impact of those messages can control our behavior can lead to overcoming those negative messages and building on the positive. On the positive side, participants will look at ways in which family can be an asset, how family members can be partners in this journey of discovery.

Because the scripture passage, which is the story of Ruth from the book of Ruth, may be too long to read at one sitting, we suggest using the summary that is found under "Insight from Scripture." The story looks at the issues of family, risk, faith, and values, particularly the values of love, loyalty, law, and caring for the poor. Note the well-known declaration of loyalty in Ruth 1:16–17.

Preparation

Make one copy for each participant:

> "Values and Lifestyle"
> "Risk Taking"

You'll need:

> handouts
> journals
> file folders
> Bibles
> pencils
> candle or cross

The Session

1. Inviting God into the Conversation

Invite God into the conversation by opening with prayer. Ask people to share the discoveries they made while working on last week's assignment, the "Assets" section (pages 7–15) of the journal. Also share the results of informational interviewing. Discuss experiences and developments of practicing faith.

2. Values and Lifestyle

One of the key concepts of this course is that God calls us to a lifestyle and a vocation.

Distribute the "Values and Lifestyle" sheet. On the sheet, participants are to circle all the items that are important to them. Out of those circled, they are to rank the top ten, in order of importance. Then, looking at their top three choices, participants are to find another person in the group who also has chosen one or more of the same items among their top three choices. The two participants spend five minutes discussing why they chose those particular values.

> God calls you to a lifestyle,
> not just a career/occupation.

Call the group back together. Ask:

- What did you discover you had in common with your partner?
- Did you circle something that surprised you?
- What values are important to you? Look at what you've written in your journal, on page 2 ("Dreaming about the Future") and in the "Assets" section. If you had to list your five most important values, what would they be? List them at the bottom of page 2. Prioritize them, if you can. Date this entry, so you can look back in later years and see if and how your values have changed.

3. Risks Exercise

Begin a discussion on risk taking by telling the participants that it is impossible to live without taking risks of some kind. What might be a risk for one person, however, is just common, ordinary behavior for another. For example, some people dread making phone calls. They fear they won't say the right thing or that they'll catch the person at a bad time. For them, phoning is a risk because it involves possible rejection. Other people don't even think about such things when making phone calls.

People differ in the kinds of risks they are willing to take. One person loves the thrill of physical risk taking and would love to bungee-jump but hates to go to parties, which involves social or interpersonal risks. Others are willing to risk social rejection but would never do anything physically risky.

Describe and discuss the four types of risks listed below. For each, ask the group to tell the upside, or payoff, of taking the risk, and then the downside. (Group members most likely will think of more upside and downside ideas than we've listed.)

- *Physical Risks*—risks of physical injury or death. The immediate payoff can be a sense of exhilaration from being in danger.
- *Financial Risks*—risks involving loss of money or financial security. The payoff can be financial success.
- *Social or Interpersonal Risks*—risks where the person may be rejected. The payoff can be the establishment of a close relationship with another person.
- *Idea Risks*—risks taken in considering new, radical, and potentially unpopular ideas. The payoff can be the intellectual excitement that comes from using one's mind in new ways.

Distribute the "Risk Taking" sheet. In the first column of blanks, participants should indicate how much they would like to do each activity by marking an X on the appropriate blank. They have five choices, ranging from "dislike a lot" to "like a lot."

For each activity the participants marked "like" or "like a lot," they are to go to the second column and put an X on the blank under the kind of risk the activity represents.

At the bottom of the right column, they then total the number of Xs.

Ask:

- Which kind of risks are you most likely to take? Which did you mark "like a lot"?
- What insights about yourself do you gain from your choices?

4. Family

Invite the participants to turn to asset #6, "Family," on page 12 in their journals. Follow the instructions. On one side, they are to list the positive messages their families bring to their lives, lifestyles, and vocations. On the other side, they list the messages they hear as negative. Note that messages refer to values and opinions held by parents and can include both nonverbal messages and those things they've heard parents say over and over again.

Discuss the positive and negative messages people hear. This can be an insightful discussion, for the experience and knowledge we gain from family can be a strong asset. Family members usually have a vested interest in their child's welfare. They also can have valuable work contacts. Participants may become discouraged by some of the items they've listed under negatives, by the "oughts" and "shoulds" presented by parents and/or other family members. In response,

consider the ways in which negatives can be seen as challenges or opportunities for change.
Ask:

- How can you approach the negatives or challenges to ensure that they won't keep you from living your call as you discern it, from taking risks, and from making choices?
- What values are of concern here? How do your values differ from those of your parents and/or other family members? How are they similar?

Discuss how parents can be partners on the career journey. Talk about ways a shift from parent role to partner role can open communication lines and improve relationships between parent and child. If you've already had the parent-participant session, invite participants to share their reactions to and learnings from the experience. If not, talk about expectations for that session. (Refer to the parent-participant session plan on p. 43.)
Ask:

- In what ways can you see your parent or guardian being a partner? In what ways can you not see that? What needs to change in your relationship to make it possible?
- For those whose parent or guardian lives in another city, talk about ways in which they might share this career journey experience. How can the parent be a long-distance partner?

5. Insight from Scripture

The Book of Ruth

Invite the participants to open their Bibles to the book of Ruth. They can follow the story line as a leader reads the following synopsis.

Because of famine in Israel during the time when the judges ruled, Naomi and her family went to live in the country of Moab. Naomi's son married Ruth, a Moabite. (The Moabites were enemies of Israel.) Naomi's and Ruth's husbands died. When the famine was over, Naomi planned to return to Israel. She encouraged Ruth to stay with her native family and gods in Moab, but Ruth had become very much attached to Naomi's family. Ruth responded with a memorable pledge of loyalty.

(At this point, invite someone to read Ruth 1:16–17, which includes "Where you go I will go, and where you stay I will stay. Your people will be my people and your God my God" [NIV].)

So Ruth moved from the enemy country of Moab to

Bethlehem. There, she went out to glean in the fields, that is, to gather the part of the harvest that was left on the ground for the poor. Gleaning was instituted by God as a way of taking care of the poor, as described in Deuteronomy 24:19–22. This was dangerous work for a young woman. Ruth caught the eye of Boaz, the foreman, who gave orders to his men not to touch her, embarrass her, or rebuke her.

After hearing of Boaz's kindness, Naomi instructed Ruth to "perfume" herself and sneak into the place where Boaz slept, in order to get him to marry Ruth. To marry her, Boaz had to go through a complicated legal procedure, which resulted in Boaz acquiring the right to marry Ruth and the right to purchase Naomi's family property, so that the names of Ruth's and Naomi's dead husbands would not disappear from their family or from the town records. (Indeed, it's complicated.)

There's one last significant element of the story. Naomi, Ruth, and Boaz were faithful to God. And, as we find out in the last two verses of the book, the union of Boaz and Ruth was part of God's plan, for they were the great-grandparents of King David.

Ask:

- What choices did Ruth have? What risks were involved with these choices?
- How do the choices men and women make today compare with those that Ruth made? Do men face different choices and risks from women?
- What role did faith have in Ruth's choices?
- What role does faith play in the choices you make?

- Do you see yourself staying near your parents or moving away? Would moving away be taking a risk for you? Why or why not?

6. Question of the Day

Complete this statement: "To really know me, you need to know that I . . ." Have participants write endings to this sentence on page 3 of their journals. Share answers.

7. Assignment

1. Continue to work on the "Assets" pages in the journal.
2. Continue to interview people using the "Informational Interview Forms."
3. Encourage everyone to conduct interviews, for the group will be discussing them next session.
4. Be on the lookout for potential mentors.

8. Closing

Discuss how to close the session. The group may want to include concerns relating to values, risk taking, and family in their closing prayer. Use a candle, cross, or whatever symbol has become a meaningful part of the group's closing worship.

Collect completed "Values and Lifestyle" and "Risk Taking" sheets for participants' file folders.

Name _____

Values and Lifestyle*

Circle the items that are important to you. Rank the top ten in order of importance.

Work in a large company with a secure job.	Make a lot of money.	Have a job where I can make the world a better place.
Create a work of art, such as a symphony, play, or painting.	Have a quiet job where there is little pressure.	Be famous and known by millions.
Have a job that gives me lots of power.	Work where I can create new things.	Work closely with people who can become close friends
Have a job that doesn't interfere with my family life.	Work where I can teach or train other people.	Work in a job where I can retire at age 50.
Work in a high-risk job environment where the demands are great but so are the rewards.	Work in a stable job where the future is fairly predictable.	Work for a boss who is friendly and thoughtful.
Work where I travel frequently.	Work at home, so I can be with my family.	Work in a family business.
Be a leading expert in something.	Make an important contribution to society.	Work by myself and be responsible to no one.
Live in a remote area, far from crowds.	Work outdoors.	Work where I can help other people every day.
Work with variety, with constantly changing activities.	Be a leader in charge of other people.	Have a job where I can work at my own pace.
Work in a job with lots of freedom, where I can come and go as I please.	Have a job where ideas are very important.	Have a job with little responsibility and little stress.

*Adapted from "Spiritmasters" for David P. Campbell's *If You Don't Know Where You're Going, You'll Probably End Up Somewhere Else* (Allen, Tex.: RCL Enterprises Inc., 1974).

Name _____

Risk Taking*

Indicate how much you would like to do each activity by marking an X on the appropriate blank. If you have indicated you would *Like* or *Like a lot* a particular activity, put an X under the kind of risk that activity represents.

	Dislike a lot	Dislike	Neutral	Like	Like a lot		Physical Risk	Financial Risk	Interpersonal or Social Risk	Idea Risk
1. Parachute out of an airplane.	—	—	—	—	—		—	—	—	—
2. Make a toast at a wedding rehearsal dinner.	—	—	—	—	—		—	—	—	—
3. Argue for wild, far-out ideas with a teacher.	—	—	—	—	—		—	—	—	—
4. Change jobs at middle age without having guaranteed security.	—	—	—	—	—		—	—	—	—
5. Drive a racing auto in a high-speed race.	—	—	—	—	—		—	—	—	—
6. Build up your own business, sell it, and begin again in a new business.	—	—	—	—	—		—	—	—	—
7. Invite someone to your church.	—	—	—	—	—		—	—	—	—
8. In a debate, take the position that the United States should outlaw all guns.	—	—	—	—	—		—	—	—	—
9. Climb a very steep cliff.	—	—	—	—	—		—	—	—	—
10. Make a short speech advocating human cloning.	—	—	—	—	—		—	—	—	—
11. Invest your money in high-risk stocks that may make you a millionaire.	—	—	—	—	—		—	—	—	—
12. Attend a party, be introduced to and mingle with people who are obviously very different from you.	—	—	—	—	—		—	—	—	—
Total for *Like* and *Like a Lot:*				—	—					

* Adapted from "Spiritmasters" for David P. Campbell's *If You Don't Know Where You're Going, You'll Probably End Up Somewhere Else* (Allen, Tex.: RCL Enterprises Inc., 1974).

CHAPTER 12

Session 5—The World of Work: Career Fields

Overview

In·this session, participants begin making connections between their interests, values, faith, and lifestyle and the world of work. The purpose of this session is not to examine individual occupations. Rather, participants will explore the ways in which their interests and preferences match specific clusters of work. The information from session 3's "Skills and Experiences" exercise will be helpful, as the six clusters of work relate to the four categories of skills: Data, People, Ideas, and Things.

First Samuel 3:1–18 is an appropriate passage for a discussion on mentor relationships. Participants will consider to whom they would go for help in discerning God's call. They will share experiences from their informational interviews.

Thinking It Through

Until now, little has been said about careers. Remind the group that in making career decisions, it is important to know yourself first. In this session and the next, as participants talk about career fields, point out connections between their career interests and their skills, interests, values, and risks—the information they've been learning about themselves.

The "Occupational Map" activity uses a well-known classification of occupations developed by John Holland at Johns Hopkins University.[1] Almost every book on careers uses Holland's classification in some form. The classification suggests that all jobs can be grouped into six clusters of occupations. On the map, surrounding the circle, you'll see the four cate-

gories used in session 3's "Skills and Experiences" exercise—Data, People, Ideas, and Things. Their location on the circle indicates their relationship to the clusters. For example, Data is closely related to the Enterprising and Conventional clusters. Generally, one can assume that the skills a person enjoys using will guide the person toward occupations in a related cluster. For example, someone whose strongest skills are with people and ideas would look at occupations in the Social and Artistic clusters.

On the "Occupations" sheet is a list of thirty occupations, five from each cluster. From this list the participants identify the eight occupations that they think they would most enjoy. For this exercise to work they must choose eight, even if they like only a few of those listed. They then transfer the eight choices to the map. Most of the time a person's choices fall in one or two clusters, often adjoining clusters. Of course, it doesn't always work out this neatly. It seems as if we always have a person whose choices are "all over the map," whose interests are too broad to categorize simply. These people have the hardest choices but the most options.

The purpose of this exercise is to spark discussion among participants about types of careers and how they relate to a person's interests, skills, and preferences. The exercise does not provide an in-depth study of careers or a comprehensive evaluation of a person's interests. Therefore, encourage the participants to be aware of learnings and questions raised in their discussions but not to draw conclusions about careers to pursue or those to avoid.

If participants have been committed to the career counseling process and have done their homework (including informational interviews), they will be aware of the multiple factors that go into deciding on a vocation. Throughout this program, they should be gaining skills that can help them examine their options.

For this session's closing, we suggest an art activity. Those who are "right-brain" will appreciate this, as they often find words limit their ability to express concepts. Moreover, in field testing we've found that those who claim no ability or interest in art usually enjoy this activity. They are willing to try something new, a different way of expressing their understandings of God. In fact, one resistant participant found her drawing expressed her relationship with God better than her words had, and she now keeps that drawing in her Bible.

Preparation

Make one copy for each participant:

"Occupations" sheet
"Occupational Map" sheet

You'll need:

handouts
journals
file folders
Bibles
pencils
colored pencils
paper (8 x 11)
clay
candle or cross

The Session

1. Inviting God into the Conversation

Open with prayer. Ask the group members to share their reflections on the career counseling process up to this point.
Ask:

- How are we doing?
- Are you comfortable sharing your thoughts, values, questions, and faith journey?
- How has God been present?
- What might help us grow in faith and support one another on this journey of discovering God's call to vocation and lifestyle?

- Are you feeling more comfortable with the practices of faith? Which are becoming a part of your life?

Finally, remind the group of the journey's process—looking at God's call and knowing yourself, then exploring the world of work. The best way to make career decisions is to know yourself first.

2. Question of the Day

Complete this statement: "The person whose job I'd most like to have is . . . " Write answers on page 3 of journals.

3. Careers on Television

Compile a list of occupations/careers that you see on television. Think of sitcoms and TV dramas. What do the various characters on the shows do?
Ask:

- What do we learn about the world of work from media—from television, movies, and music?

4. Occupational Map

The "Occupational Map" activity is designed to help participants begin to discover their preferred areas of career interests by identifying occupations they might enjoy. Explain that participants should not expect definitive results from this simple exercise. The learnings will come from their discussions, which follow the exercise.

Tell the group that the "Occupational Map" is based on the research of John Holland, who found that the happiest workers are those whose personality styles—which include values, personality traits, preferences, and interests—match their work environment. He identified and named six clusters of occupations. The name of each refers to both the personality style of the worker and the corresponding work environment:

- Realistic (Technical—work with objects, machines, tools, athletics, nature)
- Investigative (Science—observe, analyze, solve problems)
- Artistic (Arts—use imagination, creativity; work with music, drama, literature)
- Social (Social service—work closely with people; teach, counsel, cure)
- Enterprising (Business contact—work with people; lead, manage, persuade, sell)

- Conventional (Business operations—work with data, records, financial transactions)

Holland found that people who work at a job in a particular cluster have similar interests and personality styles to those who work at other jobs in the same cluster.

1. Distribute the "Occupations" sheet. Participants are to circle the eight occupations they think they would most enjoy. Someone in the group might not find any of the professions on this list appealing, but for the sake of the exercise, he must choose eight from those listed.

2. Distribute the "Occupational Map" sheet, on which the occupations from the first sheet have been grouped and placed just outside the circle nearest their appropriate cluster. On this sheet, have participants circle the same eight occupations that they circled on the first sheet. Point out the location of the skills categories—Data, People, Ideas, or Things—on the circle.

Ask:

> The question is not
> "What do you want to do when you grow up?" Rather, it is
> "What do you want to do first?"

- In which of the six job clusters did you have the most items circled? Which the second most? Which third?
- Are these clusters next to each other in the circle? (Most likely they will be, although occasionally someone will have a wide variety of interests.)
- Which skills category (Data, People, Ideas, or Things) is related to your cluster(s)? Notice that the categories overlap, that is, data skills relate to both Enterprising and Conventional; people skills relate to Enterprising, Social, and Artistic.
- Remind the group that in session 3 they completed the "Skills and Experiences" sheet, on which they discovered their preference for working with Data, People, Ideas, or Things. Does the "Occupational Map" confirm your preferences? If it does not, suggest that the participants may have an interest in acquiring skills in a new category.
- What do you discover about yourself from this exercise?

5. Informational Interviews

At this point in the career counseling process, participants should have interviewed at least one person.

If they have not, stress the importance of doing so. There is much to learn from other people's vocational experiences. And their interviewing skills will improve. Discuss the interviewing experiences.

Ask:

- What insights did you gain from the interview?
- In which job clusters are the occupations of the people you interviewed?

6. Insight from Scripture

1 Samuel 3:1–18—The Calling of Samuel

The story of God calling Samuel is rather amusing, as three times Samuel was awakened by a voice; assumed it was his mentor, Eli the priest; and obediently ran to Eli. Since Samuel did not yet know the Lord, Eli was the one to recognize that it was the Lord calling Samuel.

Invite someone to read the passage while others follow along in their Bibles.

After the reading, ask:

- If God were calling you in the same way Samuel was called, how would you react? Would you tell someone about it? Who would that person be?
- Samuel had Eli to go to for advice. Whom do you presently go to for advice? If you could have anyone in the world as your personal adviser, who would it be?
- Is there someone who recognizes the ways in which God is at work in your life, who alerts you to God's presence?
- Sometimes God calls people to do things they really do not want to do. Would you tend to ignore that call? fight against it? accept it? explore it with someone?

7. Mentor Update

Discuss how the mentor searches are progressing. Have any of the participants been able to establish mentor relationships? If the church has a mentor program, has it been helpful? Discuss ways to encourage mentor relationships. Did any of the persons interviewed have mentors?

8. Assignment

1. In the next session, participants will discuss job site visits. Suggest that they think about the occupations and job sites they'd like to visit. Encourage them to get the name of someone who has that occupation. Their informational interviews may be a source.
2. Continue getting informational interviews.
3. Continue writing in journals.
4. Continue developing mentor relationships.

9. Closing

Psalm 16 speaks of confidence in the Lord. Three verses in particular connect with the journey of discerning God's call to lifestyle and vocation: verse 2, "You are my Lord; apart from you I have no good thing"; verse 7, "I will praise the LORD, who counsels me; even at night my heart instructs me"; and verse 11, "You have made known to me the path of life" (NIV). Have someone read these verses while others follow in their Bibles.

Invite participants to use art in response to these verses. Suggest that they draw or sculpt their concept of God and their relationship to God, using colored pencils and paper or clay. When everyone has finished, ask for suggestions about how to use their creations in the closing of this session.

Collect the "Occupations" and "Occupational Map" sheets for the participants' folders.

Name _____

Occupations*

Circle the eight occupations below that you think you would most enjoy. (All thirty occupations appear on the "Occupational Map.")

Theater set designer

Social worker

Retail-sales person

Postal clerk

Landscape gardener

Day-care worker

Newspaper journalist

Public relations director

Artist or photographer

Airplane pilot

Chemist

Physical therapist

Stockbroker

Teacher or coach

Hospital administrator

Company manager or officer

Computer operator

Construction worker

Researcher

Pharmacist

Electronic-equipment designer

U.S. senator

Air traffic controller

Accountant or bookkeeper

Medical technologist

Performer

Equipment repair person

Youth minister

Farmer or forester

Legal, medical, or office secretary

*Adapted from "Spiritmasters" for David P. Campbell's *If You Don't Know Where You're Going, You'll Probably End Up Somewhere Else* (Allen, Tex.: RCL Enterprises Inc., 1974).

Name _____

Occupational Map*

On this sheet, circle the same eight occupations you circled on the "Occupations" sheet.

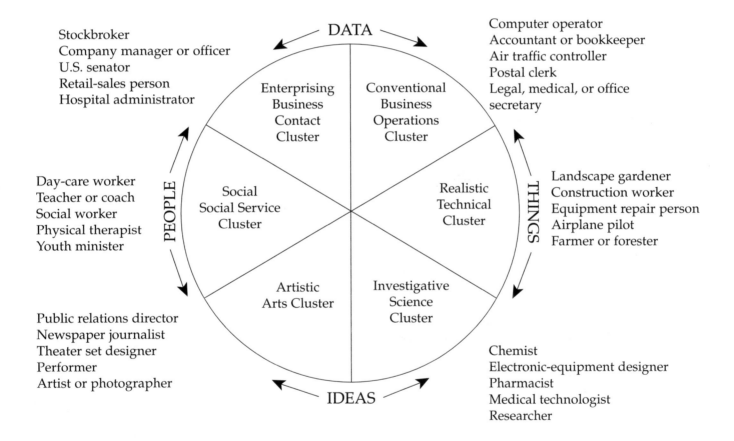

* Adapted from "Spiritmasters" for David P. Campbell's *If You Don't Know Where You're Going, You'll Probably End Up Somewhere Else* (Allen, Tex.: RCL Enterprises Inc., 1974), and from *Realizing the Dream: Career Planning for the Twenty-first Century* (Iowa City: The American College Testing Program and the National Career Development Association, 1994).

CHAPTER 13

Session 6—The World of Work: Making Plans

Overview

This is the last session of the basic career counseling program. If the group is visiting a career center for testing, all of the completed handouts, except the "Informational Interview Forms," should be sent to the center along with the applications provided by the center. The group should plan to meet two or three weeks after the center visit to discuss the reports they receive back from the center. But even if a center visit is not part of the program, in this session the participants will need to decide how they want to proceed. Will they continue to meet periodically?

In this session, participants look at one disciple's dramatic response to Jesus, potential job site visits, general work habits and life skills, tips for career planning, and an "Action Plan" to aid decision making. If you do not have enough time in the session to cover all of these issues, it might be a good idea to postpone discussion on career planning tips for an additional session. Getting back together to discuss tips might encourage group members to keep meeting.

Thinking It Through

After being together for six weeks, the group members should have learned how to talk about themselves, about their values, gifts, preferences, and faith. They should recognize that they are on a journey, a process of discovery, discernment, and growth. Some may not any more know what they want to do in life than when they started, but they should be assured that that's okay. Even though there are many unknowns ahead, everyone can make some decisions about the

steps to take. Remember, they are not alone in this endeavor. God deeply cares about them and will guide them. There are friends, mentors, family members, significant adult friends in the church, and this group, who care about them as well.

In this session you'll be discussing with participants the principle "You can't make a mistake." Even if participants choose the "wrong" job, realize they're in the "wrong" profession, or have a miserable year at one school and transfer to another, it is important for them to recognize that there are tremendous learnings and life skills gained by the very act of surviving the "wrong" choice.

The adages about history being the best teacher and learning from our mistakes are true. Many successful companies are looking for people who make mistakes, who aren't afraid to fail, because they believe that if you haven't failed, you haven't tried hard enough. If you haven't made mistakes, you haven't been willing to risk, to venture out, to grow.

So remind group members that although they will make mistakes, the point is not to perceive them as mistakes, not to interpret them as a total waste of time. Suggest they perceive their mistakes as part of their education—learning more about themselves, about people, about relationships, about a particular field, about conflict management, about coping.

Of course, it is best to have as much preparation and information as possible about career choice in order to avoid the pain of choosing a career path and regretting it. It's amazing how many people prepare for a career without having any idea what it would be like to work in that field. One young adult had wanted to be a veterinarian all her life. Her entire college program was directed toward that goal. It wasn't until her senior year of college that she interned in an animal hospital, and she was shocked to find that she couldn't stand the environment. She had always thought she'd love a career as a vet since she loved animals.

Having some idea of the work environment, finding out what people actually do in a particular field, is useful information for determining a career. That is one reason visits to job sites are so important. In this session, group members can help one another identify and connect with potential workplaces for visits.

Participants will discuss the relationship between work and faith. Until now, we've talked about lifestyles. Now we explore work style and faith style. Work style is the way you do your job; it incorporates your values and beliefs. Faith style covers more territory. It's the way you live as a believer and a disciple. A young adult who interned at a small-town television station was impressed by the work style and faith style of the station's owner and general manager. This owner succeeded in treating all employees equally. All employees were valued and knew that their jobs, no matter how menial, mattered. Now employed by a major network in New York City, this young adult is attempting to replicate the values of the local station owner. To the extent he is able,

> You can't make a mistake.

he is blurring the lines of job hierarchy—in the cafeteria, in social conversation. His faith commitment shapes his work style.

This session's scriptural insight comes from the story of Jesus walking on water toward a boatful of disciples. Peter is the one disciple who risks getting out of the boat to walk toward Jesus. The passage speaks to issues of risk and fear and the nearness of Christ, who reaches out to a follower who is sinking. You will raise two ideas for discussion: (1) the opposite of faith is fear, and (2) we ask God for a cup of water; God wants us to ask for the well. This concept suggests the magnitude of God's desire and willingness to bless us. Invite participants to reflect on these two concepts.

In the "Question of the Day" segment, participants will discuss the Outward Bound motto: "If you can't get out of it, get into it." When faced with an obstacle or a circumstance that causes fear, people often either freeze or run. The motto suggests facing the fear and dealing with the obstacle by getting "down into it," by embracing the situation, moving with faith into it and through it. The answer is not to give in but to choose not to let the obstacle win. The idea is to choose to deal with it and learn from the experience. This approach to fear should elicit interesting discussion.

Preparation

You'll need:

> journals
> file folders
> Bibles
> pencils and pens
> blank sheet of paper for each person
> candle or cross

The Session

1. Inviting God into the Conversation

Invite God into the conversation by opening with prayer. Celebrate God's presence over the past six sessions. Pray for continued presence and guidance during whatever next steps are taken.

Discuss with the group the principle "You can't make a mistake." Remind them that God calls us to activities and roles to play in the midst of what we might consider mistakes, such as being at the wrong college or in the wrong job.

Ask:

• What do you think about the idea that you can't make a mistake? Why do you think it's a key concept of the career counseling ministry program?
• Think of a situation in which you made a decision that you now think was a mistake. What did you learn from the experience? With the group, explore ways God might have been at work in that situation for each group member.

2. Job Site Visits

In the previous session, participants were asked to identify the job sites they would like to visit. On their lists should be companies that employ people in careers they are considering. They could choose the workplace of one of the adults they interviewed.

Discuss how to proceed: where to go, how to set up the job site visit, who to call. Group members can help one another with suggestions and contacts. Learning to network is an important job-hunting skill. Consider these guidelines:

1. Find a contact person in the vocation you're choosing. Tell the contact person what you're interested in seeing or doing. He or she can arrange a visit, a tour, some brief conversations with employees without disturbing the operation at the job site. Participants need to be the grateful recipients of whatever the contact can arrange.

2. Spend only ten minutes with an employee. Ten minutes is an acceptable and responsible amount of time to spend with a job holder. You can ask to speak with several employees. Be prepared to ask questions. Consider questions from the "Informational Interview Form."

3. Ask to observe for ten to fifteen minutes. You may be allowed to observe operations. Begin by asking for a short amount of time. Let the contact be the one to offer more. What often happens is the contact is delighted you have an interest in the company or vocation and offers more time and opportunities for you to learn. People are flattered to know you are interested in their vocations. Always begin, however, by asking for a minimum of their time.

4. Observe well. Notice a lot in ten minutes.

   What are people doing?
   How do they interact with each other?
   What are they wearing?
   What is the atmosphere of the workplace—fast paced? relaxed?
   What kind of work space do employees have?
   What equipment do they use?

5. Write down your observations immediately. Either outside the door or in your car, write down what you observed. Or make notes while you're observing. Later, on the same day, write your impressions. What adjectives would you use to describe the people in the career you were observing?

6. Write a thank-you note. This is a must.

3. Insight from Scripture

Matthew 14:22–33

The passage tells the dramatic story of Jesus walking on water and Peter following his example. Fear is mentioned four times. The disciples were terrified and cried out in fear. Jesus' first words were: "Take courage! It is I. Don't be afraid" (v. 27 NIV). Gutsy Peter walks toward Jesus and is fine until he sees the wind and becomes afraid.

Ask:

- How would you describe Peter's reaction to seeing Jesus?
- Where were the other disciples? We aren't told much about them, but what do you think they were thinking?
- It is often said that the opposite of faith is doubt. But according to this passage, the opposite of faith is fear. Discuss this idea. What does fear do to you? What does fear do to your faith? What do you fear?
- What does Peter request of Jesus? How does Jesus respond?

Note that Jesus often does what people ask. We are given indications throughout the New Testament that Jesus wants his followers to ask:

"If you ask anything of the Father in my name, he will give it to you. Until now you have not asked for anything in my name. Ask and you will receive, so that your joy may be complete." John 16:23–24

"Ask, and it will be given you." Luke 11:9

In the story of blind Bartimaeus (Mark 10:46–52) Jesus asks, "What do you want me to do for you?" (v. 51).

Sometimes it seems that Christians hesitate to ask God for much. Ask participants to respond to the idea "We ask God for a cup of water; God wants us to ask for the well," as implying that God has a tremendous desire and willingness to bless us.

Ask:

- What can this concept teach you about your relationship to God and about God's role in your journey of discovering what God is calling you to be and do?

4. Question of the Day

The question of the day is "What do you fear?" Give everyone an opportunity to answer. Then discuss the motto of Outward Bound, "If you can't get out of it, get into it," as a strategy for dealing with things or circumstances that you fear.

5. Work Habits and Life Skills

On page 17 in the journal is a short list of work habits that are worth developing. Discuss the habits and life skills. Suggest additions.

Ask:

- Can you think of work habits or life skills that are particularly Christian or faith oriented?
- What kind of relational or social skills do you think are helpful in the workplace?
- How does faith relate to work?
- What kind of work style and faith style would you like to develop?

6. Tips for Career Planning

On page 18 in the journal is a list of career planning tips. Invite group members to examine the list and discuss how the tips can benefit individuals at their particular stage of vocational development.

7. Action Plan

On page 19 in the journal is an "Action Plan," which is a tool to assist people in getting organized to achieve a goal. For their action plans, participants should choose something they want to do, such as apply to school, get a summer job, arrange a job site visit, or find a mentor. They are to list steps they need to take to carry out that plan. There is a sample "Action Plan" on page 20 in their journal.

Invite participants to begin working on an action plan. They can help one another. Before the end of the session, they should have some first steps listed and a date by which they will complete these steps. They can finish the action plan at home.

8. Where Do We Go from Here? Future Meetings

If a career center visit is planned, go over details. Set a date to meet, after the visit, for the group to share their career center experiences and reports. At that session, all participants should bring their reports. Plan on lively discussion as group members react to their reports.

If there is no center visit, the group needs to decide when and if it will meet again. Group members should continue informational interviews and job site visits. Mentor relationships should be continued for a period of three months, at which time a break is recommended. Both mentor and mentoree decide how to proceed after the break.

If you continue to meet, participants can discuss the jobs that interest them and identify careers they can eliminate from consideration. They can continue to explore God's call to a lifestyle as well as a vocation and to share experiences with the practices of faith. And they can continue to examine the role of family and friends in their vocation, lifestyle, and further education.

Group members can also explore colleges, summer opportunities, part-time job opportunities, full-time job possibilities, interviews, volunteer activities, and church involvement. Chapter 14 suggests ways to carry on this career counseling ministry beyond the six-session period.

9. Closing Worship

Gather in a circle. Invite participants to share ways in which they have invited God into the conversation and what they have discovered about God, themselves, their lives, and their futures. Since this is the last session, consider blessing one another with affirmations. Distribute a blank sheet of paper and pencils or pens to each member. Participants write their names at the top of the paper. Then they pass the paper to the person on the right. That person writes something affirming about the person named and passes the paper to the person on his or her right, who adds another affirmation. When the papers reach their owners, everyone has a blessing in writing.

Another way to do this blessing is to tape the blank sheet to each person's back. People mingle, writing affirmations on each other's papers.

Group members may have other suggestions for closing.

CHAPTER 14

Staying on the Journey

The key is to stay in conversation with God.

It seems that just when group members are getting comfortable sharing with one another discoveries about themselves and their faith journeys, the six weeks are over. The group is probably just beginning to gel. Participants have learned to trust one another and to turn to each other for opinions and advice. It would be a shame to call it quits.

During session 6, group members were to decide the future of their career counseling group. They are the ones to decide how often to meet and the activities and discussions they need. They can meet monthly or biweekly or make that decision each time they get together. Additional sessions are less structured; for example, they have no specific activity sheets. They would allow time for each participant to give updates on career thinking, job hunting and interviewing; plans for further education; plans for summer and part-time jobs; and learnings and experiences growing in faith.

There's also a good chance participants won't be able to cover everything called for in the six sessions within the given time frame. With additional sessions, members can have time for more informational interviews and visits to job sites. They can have additional opportunities for developing mentor relationships and for exploring ways in which parents or guardians can be partners in the exploration of God's call.

Additional sessions also afford time for relaxed conversation, in which participants and leaders can continue sharing their experiences with practices of faith. They can continue discussion about God, faith, work, and lifestyle. They can continue exploring God's word through Bible study. (Eight passages are included in this chapter.) They can worship, play, and keep traveling the journey of discovery.

Participants would continue bringing their journals to additional sessions and would encourage one another to continue journaling. They may have new entries to make on the "Assets" pages. They could spend time discussing the tips for career planning on page 18 in their journals.

In additional sessions, to keep the group focused on sharing discoveries, use the following questions for discussion:

1. What have I learned? about myself? about God? about my faith? about the world of work?
2. What skills do I need for the journey of life? Consider work habits, life skills, practices of faith, and social skills.
3. What do I still need to do to prepare for career, college, jobs, interviews? to make decisions? to work on an action plan?
4. What goals—general and specific—can I set? For example, what goals can I set in relation to vocation? to skill development? to school? to family? to lifestyle, faith, practices, church involvement, values, and service or mission opportunities?
5. At present, what is God calling me to be and do?

Groups can plan trips—to college campuses, military bases, job fairs, and career seminars. If the group visits an interdenominational career center or other testing center, group members should meet as soon as they receive reports from the center.

The career counseling program is an excellent entry point for connecting people to the life of the church. Group members and their leaders and mentors can participate in a mission project or other ministry. Such involvement can help individuals make active church membership a part of their lifestyle.

An Additional Question of the Day

One question remains to be answered in the journals, #7 on page 3. Complete this sentence by listing as many things as come to mind: "I am . . . " Use nouns, adjectives, whatever. In an additional session, encourage participants to write answers on page 3 in their journals. Suggest that they continue to add answers in the future.

Scripture Passages for Exploration

1. *Acts 9:1–22 (Saul's conversion):* Saul's conversion was dramatic—flashing light from heaven, the voice of Jesus (who had already been crucified), Saul blinded for three days.

QUESTIONS FOR DISCUSSION
- What was Saul's call from God? How did he receive it? What was his response?
- Review exactly what happened to Saul after receiving his call.
- What challenges did Saul face (see 9:23–30)?
- What in Saul's experience and commitment resonates with your journey of faith?

2. *Exodus 3:1–4:17 (call of Moses):* Moses' encounter with God at the burning bush was dramatic. God called Moses to bring the Israelites out of Egypt. Moses raised objections five times.

QUESTIONS FOR DISCUSSION
- Find the five times Moses raised doubts about carrying out what God called him to do. What was God's response each time Moses spoke his concerns?
- In what ways do you find yourself doubting God's call or doubting yourself?
- What do you learn about God from this passage?

3. *Luke 4:16–21 (Jesus' call):* After Jesus' baptism, at which the voice from heaven said, "You are my Son, the Beloved; with you I am well pleased" (Luke 3:22), Jesus was led by the Spirit into the wilderness for forty days, where he was tempted. Then, in the synagogue, he stated his call, reading familiar words from the scroll of the prophet Isaiah. He astonished those in the synagogue by claiming to be the fulfillment of that scripture.

QUESTIONS FOR DISCUSSION
- What was Jesus' call?
- Why is it significant that Jesus' call and the words of Isaiah are the same?
- What do you learn about Jesus from this passage?
- What does Jesus' call tell you about God's intention for the world?
- How do we fit in all this? In what ways do Jesus' call and our calls mesh?

4. *Romans 12:1–2 (practice of faith, discernment):* Part of the practice of worship is the practice of offering. In Romans the offering is a "living sacrifice," which refers to our entire being, including our lifestyle and vocation. In chapter 3 of this book we talk about the practice of embodying, which is what we do to live out our faith. Romans 12:2 gives us an important clue about embodying, or living in response to God. The clue is that we need to be transformed by the renewal of our minds, which results in our being able to discern the will (and call) of God.

QUESTIONS FOR DISCUSSION
- What practice of faith is talked about in verses 1–2?
- What is a "living sacrifice" (v. 1)?
- According to the passage, how can we know what God's will is?
- What does it mean to be conformed to the world?
- What transformation is Paul talking about?
- What does this say to you about your life?

5. *Psalm 139 (the presence of God):* The psalmist writes of an incredible closeness with God. The Psalm can be divided into sections for meditation—verses 1–6, 7–12, 13–16, 17–18, 19–22, and 23–24. (Verses 19–22 seem to be an intrusion in the midst of the writer's outpouring of devotion. Yet it makes sense that this passionate believer would abhor those who rise up against God.)

QUESTIONS FOR DISCUSSION
- What do you learn about God from this psalm?
- What do you think it means to be "fearfully and wonderfully made" (v. 14)?
- Throughout the career sessions, we've been inviting God into the conversation and talking about connecting faith and life, faith and work. In what ways does this psalm relate to these concepts?

6. *Hebrews 10:24–25 (encouraging one another, accountability):* Verse 25a is suited for the consideration of additional career sessions—"Let us not give up meeting together" (NIV).

QUESTIONS FOR DISCUSSION
- What does it mean to "spur one another on" (v. 24 NIV)?
- How can you spur one another on to love and good deeds?
- Do we as Christians or group members have a responsibility to encourage one another?
- Should we be accountable to one another? in what ways?
- Why is meeting together so important?

7. *Philippians 3:12–14 (forgetting the past, pressing on toward the goal):* Paul speaks about the life-consuming goal of God's call and how he presses on to "take hold of that for which Christ Jesus took hold of" him (NIV). Verse 13b, "forgetting what lies behind," connects to the career program's principle "You can't make a mistake." The important thing is to move forward with being about God's call.

QUESTIONS FOR DISCUSSION
- What does this passage tell you about how you should live your life?
- In light of this passage, how might you think differently about your career or your career search?
- What is the "prize" mentioned in verse 14? Does it refer to something in the present? future? both?

8) *Matthew 10:1–20 (the sending of the twelve disciples):* Chapter 10 is full of Jesus' instructions on how the disciples are to fulfill their calling. The disciples left their occupations to follow Jesus. It will be interesting to see what youth and young adults recall about the careers of the followers of Jesus.

QUESTIONS FOR DISCUSSION
- What careers were represented among the Twelve whom Jesus called?
- Were there others who followed Jesus? Who were they? Name some. Do we know their occupations?
- Were these people similar? Did Jesus have a variety of personalities and backgrounds present with him? Does this suggest anything in regard to diversity?
- List Jesus' instructions to his followers. List the warnings Jesus gives. What assurance are the disciples given? See verse 20.
- In what ways does Jesus tell us how to work, live, and fulfill our callings? What assurance does Jesus give us?

Challenge to Participants: Keep It Going

The responsibility for keeping the career group going belongs to the participants. If group members have developed ownership in the program, they are more likely to care what happens both to the group members individually and to the career counseling ministry itself.

The ministry of career counseling and vocational identity is much needed in local churches. It is a ministry worth the time and effort, for we see amazing transformations in the lives and attitudes of both youth and young adults. One of our favorite stories comes from the Career Development Center of the Southeast in Decatur, Georgia.

Shawn was an eleventh grader whose parents had sent him to the career center. It was obvious from his demeanor that he did not want to be there. His parents had been on his case about his lack of ambition, his procrastination about doing homework, and his messy room. Perhaps these well-meaning parents had hoped the center might cure him of his "problems."

Shawn projected an image of low self-esteem. The world seemed to be telling him he was not okay and needed fixing. Shawn's test results revealed that he was a person who did not jump to conclusions, whose thinking was open to possibilities, and who put off making decisions for fear that deciding too quickly could lead to error.

The counselor explained these results to Shawn, telling him that people like him make good attorneys, troubleshooters, and mediators, because they walk into a situation with an open mind and are willing to be patient while seeking answers.

Suddenly, the sullen Shawn lifted his head, looked the counselor in the eyes for the first time, and said, "So, are you trying to tell me it's okay to be me?" Since he had been perceiving himself as "not okay," he did not value himself. It was hard for Shawn to believe in God's unconditional love, for he assumed God was judging him the same way that he perceived the world and his parents to be judging him.

By the time Shawn left the center, he was a changed person. The counselor told us that even though he was delighted with Shawn's transformation, he regretted that Shawn was not part of a career counseling group where he could receive affirmation from peers who were on the same journey of self-discovery, and where he could experience the unconditional love of God evident in a community of faith.

The joy of career counseling ministry is seeing the shift in attitude from fear and anxiety to confidence and joyful expectancy as youth and young adults strengthen their faith and grow in their understanding that life is lived in response to God's call and that God has created them with unique gifts to carry out that call. There is definitely a difference in the outlook of those who believe that ultimately God has a purpose for their lives. Life will be full of struggles and disappointments, but knowing that God provides an abundant, meaningful life makes it all worthwhile.

Though her life was tragically short, Cassie Rene Bernall had that confident outlook on life. It has been reported that Cassie was the seventeen-year-old Columbine High School junior who, when asked by the gunman, "Do you believe in God?" replied yes and was killed. Her confidence and faithfulness became known when her friend Amanda revealed a note Cassie had written the night before her death and handed to Amanda on the morning of the shooting. The last line read:

> P.S. Honestly, I want to live completely for God. It's hard and scary, but totally worth it.[1]

It is through the words and lives of today's teenagers and young adults that the goodness and love of our generous God will be made known. We are bold enough to believe that the work we do, the work you will do, in career counseling ministry will significantly impact the lives and vocations of many youth and young adults. Even more boldly, we believe that all of us—leaders, participants, and parents—together can impact the work world and bring about the revolution of God's grace and love.

APPENDIX 1*

Journal

*Listen to what your life is saying
to you and take notes on it.*

This is your personal journal.
Remember to date your entries so you can see the course your life takes.

Take Note: This Is Important!

1. You are created in God's image. You are a person of infinite worth.

2. God is your partner in exploring, discovering, and living life.

3. You are co-creator with God. God created the world and invites you to continue that creative work, to help make the world what God intended it to be.

4. The key is to stay in conversation with God.

5. You can't make a mistake.

6. The question is not "What do you want to do when you grow up?" Rather, it is "What do you want to do first?"

7. Career is not just about doing; it's also about being. What is God calling you to *be* and *do?*

8. God calls you to a lifestyle, not just a career/occupation.

9. God's call is discovered in community (the we-ness of the call).

To be created in the image of God is to reflect God's goodness, love, and wisdom.

"God has determined in Jesus Christ not to be God without us."[1]
—Stacy Johnson

We are most ourselves when we are closest to God in whose image we are made.

Dreaming about the Future

List things—events, activities, people, values—that you hope will be a part of your future.

"Before you tell your life what you intend to do with it, listen for what it intends to do with you."[2]
—Parker Palmer

Creator and Generous God,
We are grateful you did not choose to be alone but called a world into being where you are working out your purposes through us, your beloved.

Our deepest happiness is knowing we are becoming who God created us to be.

Questions of the Day

These are the "questions of the day" from the sessions.

1. When you were a little kid, what was one of the things you wanted to be when you grew up?

2. I can't imagine life without . . .

3. What adjectives would you use to describe yourself?

4. To really know me, you need to know that I . . .

5. Whose job would you most like to have?

6. What do you fear?

7. Complete this sentence by listing as many things as come to mind: I am . . . (Use nouns, adjectives, whatever.)

"Spirituality helps us to think through the many selves that walk around in our skin."[3]
—Walter Brueggemann

Write about what it feels like when you're hopeless, helpless, or feel empty.

Write about how it feels to see the hand of God reaching to help you.

Called by God

What does it mean to be called by God?

I feel God is calling me to . . .

Ways to listen for God—List practices of faith you want to try

Gracious God,
  Show me who I am
and what you want me
to do with my life.
How are you moving
me in this decision?
How will I become
the person you are
calling me to be?

It's okay not to be certain
that you are doing God's
will. If we could be sure,
there would be no need
for faith.

Allow God to do something
through you today.

"Look to see what God is
already doing, so you can
join it."[4]
—Sister Elizabeth Liebert

Practices of Faith

Practices of faith are the things we do to know God better and to live intentionally as followers of Jesus Christ. Practices put us in a position to make space for God, to be aware of God's presence, to "hear" God. On this page and the next is a list of practices you may want to become a part of your lifestyle.

Prayer
Centering prayer
Breath prayers—phrase/word
Prayer of the heart—pray without ceasing by repeating a prayer phrase throughout the day. To discover your phrase: relax; relax your mind; visualize Jesus; find your name for God; bring together your name for God and your desire.
Prayer walk
Walking a labyrinth
Lectio divina (holy reading)
Dialoguing with God
Examen
Praying your life line
Engaging the body in prayer—dance, movement
Drawing, painting

Meditation
Journal writing
Worship
Observances of the liturgical year: Advent, Lent
Sabbath keeping
Embodying

Presence
Bible study
Practice of the presence of God (cultivation of awareness)
Encountering God through nature
Instruction
Tithing

Discernment
Sharing faith
Hospitality
Healing
Solitude (stillness, silence, contemplation)
Fasting

Feasting
Spiritual direction/spiritual friends
Simplicity
Creating memories
Praise
Thanksgiving

The goal of the Christian life is intimacy with God through Christ.

"I am the LORD *your God, who teaches you what is best for you, who directs you in the way you should go."*
—Isaiah 48:17 (NIV)

Confession
Intercession
Petition
Blessing
Hymn singing
Affirmation of faith

Baptism
The Lord's Supper
Confirmation
Ordination
Stewardship
Preaching

Pilgrimage
Gratitude
Forgiveness
Compassion
Justice
Ministry

Service
Study
Healing
Recreation, play
Renewal opportunities
Retreats
Corporate discernment (church committees)

*What do you need
to change
in order to
make more space
for God in
your life?*

*Practices mold
us and shape us
into the people
God wants us to be.*

Your Assets

Skills, Gifts, Talents, Abilities

Fill out the form titled "Discovering Your Gifts" (p. 85) to help expand your understanding of skills and talents. Add to the list other skills, talents, things you can do. Fill out a "Skills and Experiences" sheet (p. 79).

1. Which of the gifts you checked and listed do you see as valuable?

2. Which skills and gifts are useful for occupations you may choose?

3. Which skills and gifts will be useful throughout life?

4. Which skills or gifts might other people pay you to teach them?

5. Which skills and gifts do you enjoy using?

6. What new skills and gifts can you add to the lists?

Inventory your assets and put them in God's hands.

*In seeking to follow God's call,
you discover gifts
within yourself
you never knew
you had.*

Motivation

1. Complete the following sentence:
   In the area of _____, I am highly motivated. In which other areas are you motivated?

"Be still, and know that I am God!"
—Psalm 46:10

2. What motivates you? Where does your motivation come from?

Some see the glass half full; some see it half empty. God sees it full.

3. How hard are you willing to work?

Listen for the still, small voice.

4. People tend to be as motivated as the people close to them. What is the level of motivation of your friends? family? other?

"I came that they may have life, and have it abundantly."
—John 10:10

Friends

People tend to become like their friends in attitudes, actions, and opinions. This works both ways. Friends also can become like you! In what ways are your friends an asset? In what ways are they not?

Talk to a friend about your sense of call.

It is impossible to have a relationship with someone without communication. Likewise, it is not possible to have a relationship with God and not communicate with God.

To what or to whom are you loyal?

Education

To make your education an asset:

1. Study something that you enjoy.

   List things that you enjoy studying, classes you enjoy, areas that interest you.

2. Go to the best educational institution that (1) you can afford and (2) to which you can be admitted.

   List colleges you'd like to attend. List them according to "likelihood of getting in":
   - reaches (not likely to be accepted)

   - good prospects (good chance of getting in)

   - sure things (you'll get in)

3. Wherever you go, try to do well. Take advantage of every course you take. Remember, you can't make a mistake. Write yourself an encouraging word!

"Make me to know you ways, O LORD;
  teach me your paths.
Lead me in your truth,
and teach me,
  for you are the God of my salvation;
  for you I wait all the day long."
  —Psalm 25:4–5

"Grace is having your deepest longings and needs answered when you can't do anything about it."[5]
  —Andrew Dreitcer

Lifelong Learning

Education happens in and out of schools. Learning happens everywhere. Your mind is a tremendous asset. Just like the body, the mind needs exercise and conditioning. Keeping your mind in shape makes you a more interesting and marketable person. Stay active mentally. Read, ask questions, try new things, take on challenges, move out of your comfort zone once in a while. Be around people who are better educated than yourself.

1. In what situations can you see yourself enjoying learning? How do you learn best?

2. Write down some ways you can continue to educate yourself.

3. Read a book or magazine that is "not you," something you'd never think of reading.

Hear God saying to you:
"What do you want
me to do for you?"

"I bless the LORD *who*
gives me counsel;
  in the night also my
heart instructs me. . . .
You show me the path of life.
  In your presence there
is fullness of joy;
  in your right hand
are pleasures
    forevermore."
      —Psalm 16:7, 11

Family

Family has a powerful influence on your future, choice of college, choice of career. Most people receive a set of "shoulds" or "oughts" from parents and family, both positive and negative. Here's a sample: "You should only do what's safe"; "You should go into the family business"; "You should attend such-and-such university"; "You should care about others."

1. Below, under "Positives," list the positive messages you receive (or have received) from your family. Under "Negatives," list the negative messages.

Positives   Negatives

2. What skills can your family members teach you?

A Tip (should you have children): For good reason, parents often tell children they hate to go to work, saying they'd rather be with their children. This is affirming for children, but it may suggest that work is "bad." Think about how you talk about your work. Consider ways to speak positively, so that children will grow up with healthy values concerning work and vocation.

God calls us to bring Christ to life in one another.

We need to create space for God in order to listen for God. Think about how you might offer sacred space to your parents or other family members.

Experiences

1. Think about your experiences; not just your job experiences but life experiences—problems faced, accomplishments, travel, changes, moves. What have you learned from these? What skills and abilities have you gained?

Recognize the ways God blesses you.

"Give thanks in all circumstances; for this is the will of God in Christ Jesus for you."
—1 Thessalonians 5:18

2. Think of a really bad time or experience. How did you cope? What helped you get through it?

3. What leadership experiences have you had?

4. At this point in your life, what have you learned about yourself (about how you relate to people; how you handle challenges, disappointments, barriers; how you make decisions; your faith style; your work style; your values; your fears; your willingness to risk; what to do next—the next step)?

5. What's important to you in life? What do you think will be important to you in five years? ten years? What will be the same? What will be different?

Faith Experiences

1. When have you experienced God in your life?

How has God been messing with your life?

God is faithful.

2. What events have strengthened your faith?

Ask yourself: How much do you really believe in the promises of God—peace, reconciliation, healing, love, unity?

3. List things you plan to do now and in the future to nurture your faith.

4. List significant experiences you've had in the church, for example, in worship, study, mission, service, or fellowship.

5. List ways you'd like to be involved in the church in the future.

Personal Characteristics and Health

1. List personal characteristics and attributes, things you've got going for you.

God delights in you.

"Self-care is never a selfish act—it is simply good stewardship of the only gift I have, the gift I was put on earth to offer to others."[6]
　　—Parker J. Palmer

"No one can make you feel inferior without your consent."
　　—Eleanor Roosevelt

2. How can you improve your appearance? Your health? Your interpersonal skills?

Interests

Identifying your interests is a primary factor in empowering you to follow your dream and find a career and lifestyle that fulfill who you are and what God is calling you to be and do.

1. Quickly list everything you can think of that interests you.

2. When you walk into a book or magazine store, which section do you go to first? What other sections do you visit?

3. Imagine that you are going to a mall that has every kind of store that could exist. In which stores would you enjoy spending time browsing?

4. When you pick up a newspaper, which sections do you read? Why?

5. What do you enjoy talking about? If you were stuck on a plane for eight hours and the person next to you wanted to talk, what subjects would make the time fly by?

6. When you browse the Web, what topics do you like to enter? What Web sites do you visit?

7. Someone has offered to pay you to go anywhere in the world to study for three weeks at any university/school/training program. Where would you go? What would you study?

Find what you really love to do and figure out a way to get paid for it.

General Work Habits and Life Skills

1. Here is a list of habits worth developing for work and life. Suggest additions. Write them down.

>   Being on time
>   Getting along well with co-workers
>   Listening
>   Hearing and carrying out instructions
>   Selling yourself (being positive without bragging)
>   Being interested in others and what interests them
>   Being a visionary
>   Developing leadership skills
>   Caring about others
>   Being responsible

2. What relational or social skills would be helpful in your career or simply as an asset to your personality?

Pursue your passion and put passion in your pursuit.

Gracious and loving God, Fill my mind and imagination with images of your divine purpose for me. Fill my heart with your love so that I may serve you and others.

Career Planning Tips

1. Invite God into the conversation at every step. Seek wisdom, patience, and guidance.

2. Pay attention—to people you meet and to careers people have. Get in the habit of asking people questions. It will increase your social skills as well as give you information about potential careers.

3. Identify your distinctive qualities or experiences. If fifteen people were applying for the same job, what would make you stand out?

4. Learn to sell yourself. You'll need this ability for résumés and job interviews. In an interview, be prepared to hear, "Tell me about yourself."

5. Prepare thoroughly for job interviews. Research the company before the interview. Ask good questions. Say what you want to do for the organization rather than "I'll do anything."

6. Seek volunteer activities, leadership experiences, and career-related jobs and internships. Employers look for these on résumés.

7. Seek internships. Internships offer incredible benefits:
   • you find out if you really are interested in the career;
   • you develop specific skills;
   • you make contacts networking;
   • interns often bring new ideas to the organization/company;
   • employers usually prefer to hire former interns.

8. For college students, major in something you enjoy. You'll get better grades and maintain a higher level of interest in and commitment to your education. Employers are more interested in skills than majors.

9. Take advantage of career services. Some high schools and colleges offer career courses.

10. Join associations and read trade journals in your field of interest.

11. Go for your passion. Don't just look for job vacancies. Discover your interests, what you love to do, and aggressively seek the vocations in which you can flourish. Practice your creativity: take your top two interests and invent a job that uses both.

12. Think big! Have vision. What does the world most need from you?

   Add additional tips as you discover them:

"The place God calls you to is the place where your deep gladness and the world's deep hunger meet."[7]
   —Frederick Buechner

Vocation is not "a goal to be achieved but . . . a gift to be received."[8]
   —Parker Palmer

"Keep a space where God can let something truly new take place."[9]
   —Henri Nouwen

Action Plan

Identify the activity or action that needs to be taken (for example, applying to schools, finding a summer job, deciding on a career path).

1. On a sheet of paper, list all the steps you need to take. Leave space between each step, for you may think of additional steps.

2. Arrange the steps in the order they need to be done.

3. Are there steps with which you'll need help? Getting the help you need may involve another step or set of steps.

4. Determine the date by which each step needs to be done. Setting dates for each step keeps you from procrastinating.

5. List the dates on a calendar.

6. Checkpoints: Identify dates for checking on the progress of the steps. This keeps you on task.

7. Keep the action plan in a place where you will look at it frequently. Put it in several places: in your appointment calendar or day book, in your journal, in your Bible or devotional book, in a file folder on the activity. Refer to it often.

8. Evaluate your efforts. Make notes after you have completed the action. Indicate what you were proud you did, what was difficult, and how you handled the difficulties. Note what you would do differently next time.

"Each time a door closes, the rest of the world opens up. All we need to do is stop pounding on the door that just closed, turn around—which puts the door behind us—and welcome the largeness of life that now lies open."[10]

—Parker J. Palmer

A Sample Action Plan

Goal: Finding a Summer Job

1. List steps:

    Find out what jobs are available.

    Decide location (city, country, area)—at home or away.

    Call people to solicit suggestions about where to work.

    Make a list of employers to call.

    Call employers and ask for applications/interviews.

    Fill out application.

    Get dates of family vacation week.

2. Arrange steps in order:

    Decide location.

    Get dates of family vacation week.

    Find out what jobs are available.

    Call people to solicit suggestions about where to work.

    Make a list of employers to call.

    Call employers and ask for applications/interviews.

    Fill out application.

3. Need help finding a list of jobs that are available:

    Ask people from church.

    Ask friends.

    Check the Internet.

4. The date each step needs to be done:

Decide location	February 15
Get dates of family vacation week	March 1
Find out what jobs are available	March 15
Call people for suggestions about where to work	March 17
Make a list of employers to call	March 20
Call employers and ask for applications/interviews	March 24
Fill out and submit applications	March 30

5. Transfer dates to calendar.

6. Checkpoint dates: every Monday in February and March.

"God has been messing with you all your life. God loved you way before you took your first breath. God has been revealing Godself to you. God has been faithful throughout, inviting you into relationship."[11]
—Ben Campbell Johnson

APPENDIX 2*

A Spiritualilty Retreat

This spirituality retreat design can be used with the career counseling group or with any group of youth or young adults who already know one another or have begun to meet regularly. It's not designed to be used as a first meeting, for getting acquainted, or for outreach. It works best with a small group, fewer than fifteen people.

This particular retreat took place at a lake house with a group of seven young people. It began on a Friday evening and concluded on Saturday at mid-afternoon. The retreat design is very flexible. Time can be extended for any activity.

Purpose of the Retreat

To retreat, get away, and experience a change of pace, a slower pace.

To experience various practices of faith.

To grow spiritually by being willing to "let God in," to listen for God.

Friday

Introduction

(7:15 P.M.)

We explained the purpose of the retreat and talked about our expectations and the willingness to try something new. We began with a simple exercise of sharing. We invited participants to choose one of the following experiences to share:

1. Tell the group about something you tried that was new to you. Was the experience positive or negative?
2. Tell us about something that is causing stress in your life right now.
3. Tell us about a person, place, or event that has helped you feel closer to God.

Resource Person

(7:45 P.M.)

In our retreat, we were fortunate to have a lay leader who was a massage therapist. She shared her career journey and her faith journey and gave us a brief talk on stress relief and healthy living.

Guided Imagery

(8:15 P.M.)

We did a guided imagery exercise, in which participants were led to imagine their own place of peace and healing. We used an audiotape by Bernie Siegel, author of *Love, Medicine, and Miracles* and director of ECAP (Exceptional Cancer Patients).[1] The voice of Siegel on tape served as the leader of the exercise. (Several resources on meditation include guided imagery exercises. Some, such as Walt Marcum's *Living in the Light*,[2] use scripture passages as the setting for the guided imagery.)

We debriefed the exercise, using the following questions:

1. Was it easy or difficult to "get into" this exercise? Did you stay with it or drift off? (It's okay to fall asleep—it's an indication of relaxation).
2. Describe your experience.
3. What did you learn about yourself?

Spiritual Growth Discussion

(8:45 P.M.)

We spent twenty minutes exploring how we grow spiritually. We talked about forms of prayer, ways to pray, when to pray, and experiences of prayer.

We introduced the practices of meditation, solitude, and talking with a spiritual friend. Participants used their journals from the career counseling program. We provided additional blank pages.

Fifteen minute break.

Massage, Solitude, and Time with a Spiritual Friend

(9:30 P.M.)

Participants signed up for thirty-minute slots in three activities—a massage, solitude, and time with one of the leaders to talk about spiritual growth or whatever was on their minds. The only activity that was required was the thirty-minute period of solitude. Several participants worried that there was no way they could survive thirty minutes alone, without television or friends.

For the solitude time, participants were given the "Guide to Scripture Meditation" (see p. 132). They found spaces to be alone in the lake house and on the porch. They were encouraged to listen for God in the silence.

Guided Meditation and Prayer

(11:00 P.M.)

We gathered on the dock on a bright, moonlit night. All participants found a spot where they could lie on their backs. They had to be touching someone (either with arm, hand, foot, or leg) to represent our connectedness and communion with God and one another.

The leader invited them to close their eyes, to relax their muscles, starting with their feet and moving up to their faces. They were to pay attention to their breathing, to think of breathing in God's love and breathing out conflict, breathing in God's peace, breathing out hatred.

Then the leader slowly read a guided imagery meditation on the pearl of great price (Matthew 13:45–46) from Walt Marcum's *Living in the Light.* In the meditation, the participants imagine encountering Jesus on a seashore, where he gives them a precious gift. Each person imagines and discerns what that particular gift is.

Because of the late hour, we did not debrief this exercise. We closed with an emptying prayer in which the leader invited everyone to empty their minds, to be silent, to dwell in that silence, and to listen for God.

Saturday

Morning Prayers

(9:00 A.M.)

After breakfast, we gathered for morning prayers. We first talked about the various forms of prayer we'd experienced at the retreat. We then began prayer with a centering prayer, in which the leader instructed everyone to focus on the center of their bodies, to release tension and be at peace, and to sense peace flowing out from their centers. The group members talked about prayer concerns; we prayed; we talked more and prayed more.

Guided Meditation on the Dock

(9:30 A.M.)

We returned to the dock for another guided meditation. All participants found a spot to lie on their backs, once again touching another person to represent our supporting and being supported by one another. As part of the instructions to relax, the leader told group members to feel the warmth of the sunlight and to experience God as light. The meditation was based on John 15:1–8, the vine and the branches; it suggested that we are the branches connected to one another and to the true vine, Jesus Christ.

Massage, Solitude, and Time with a Spiritual Friend

(10:00 A.M.)

This ninety-minute session was a repeat of the Friday-evening session with the choice of three activities: massage, solitude, and a visit with a leader who served as a spiritual friend.

Take It Home

(1:30 P.M.)

After lunch and a little time for recreation, we gathered to process the experience, to discuss what knowledge and experience individuals would take with them as a result of the retreat. We used the following questions:

1. What have you learned about stress and stress reduction?
2. What did you experience during the guided meditations?
3. What scripture passages did you find especially meaningful?
4. In what ways did you listen for God?
5. What practices of faith do you want to continue: journal writing? solitude? meditation? prayer? others?
6. How can we encourage one another in spiritual growth?

Closing

(2:15 P.M.)

We asked the group members how they wanted to close. They chose to return to the dock, sit in a circle, read John 15:7–8, and pray—anyone could pray at any time.

A spirituality retreat such as this can be one of the most relaxing experiences a group of young adults or youth can have. Ours was a short retreat. We wished we had planned to stay longer. The schedule could be more relaxed if there were more time. Not everyone would be able to invite a massage therapist, but we suggest you look for resource people in your congregation who can share their gifts—related to reducing stress or helping with spiritual formation.

Guide to Scripture Meditation

1. Devotional Reading

Read the Bible from the perspective of asking what God has to say to you right now through this passage. God speaks through the scriptures. What do you feel God is saying to you?

2. Meditating on Scripture

Read a passage, then reread it, looking for things that "jump out" at you. It may be a word, phrase, or image. It may be a thought provoked by the text. This word, phrase, image, or thought serves as your starting point. Then begin to free-associate, thinking about that word, phrase, image, or thought, seeing where it may lead. In this process, God can speak to you through the scripture.

3. Relational Bible Study

Read the passage for what it has to say about relationships. Focus on four levels of relationships: (1) with God, (2) with ourselves, (3) with other people, and (4) with the world.

Suggested Scriptures for Meditation

Psalms 5; 8; 18:1–3, 16; 23; 25; 27; 31:1–5; 37:1–11; 42; 46; 51; 86; 90; 91; 100; 103; 116; 118; 121; 130; 133; 139; 143; 145; 146

Matthew 6:9–13	Matthew 6:33	Mark 8:34	Mark 9:35
Luke 4:18–19	Luke 10:27	Luke 11:9	Luke 18:13b
John 1:1–5	John 1:14	John 3:16	John 4:14
John 6:35	John 9:4–5	John 9:38	John 10:14–15
John 11:25	John 14:1–3	John 14:6	John 15:5
Acts 2:17	Romans 1:16	Romans 3:22–24	Romans 6:4, 8
Romans 7:15	Romans 8:28	Romans 8:37–39	Romans 10:9
Romans 12:1–3	1 Corinthians 3:16	1 Corinthians 6:19–20	1 Corinthians 10:13
1 Corinthians 12:12–13	2 Corinthians 5:17	2 Corinthians 5:19	2 Corinthians 12:9
Galatians 3:28	Galatians 5:22	Ephesians 1:9–10	Ephesians 4:1–5
Ephesians 4:11–12	Ephesians 5:1	Philippians 1:27	Philippians 3:13b–14
Philippians 4:4–7	Philippians 4:13	1 Thessalonians 5:16	1 Thessalonians 5:23–24
2 Thessalonians 2:16–17	1 Timothy 1:15, 17	1 Timothy 4:9	Hebrews 12:1–3
Hebrews 13:5–6	Hebrews 13:8	Hebrews 13:20–21	1 John 1:9
1 John 3:1–2	1 John 3:11	1 John 3:16	1 John 4:7, 10
1 John 4:19	3 John 1:11	Revelation 3:20	Revelation 21:1–4
Revelation 22:13			

APPENDIX 3*

Recommended Reading

General Resources on Career and Call

Atwell, Judy. *This Call's for You: A Christian Vocation Workbook for Congregations.* Louisville, Ky.: Office of Enlistment Services, Presbyterian Church (U.S.A.), 1993.

Barkley, Nella. *How to Help Your Child Land the Right Job (without Being a Pain in the Neck).* New York: Workman Publishing, 1993.

Bluestein, Jane, comp. *Mentors, Masters and Mrs. MacGregor: Stories of Teachers Making a Difference.* Deerfield Beach, Fla.: Health Communications, Inc., 1995.

Bolles, Richard Nelson. *What Color Is Your Parachute?* Berkeley, Calif.: Ten Speed Press, published annually.

Campbell, David P. *If You Don't Know Where You're Going, You'll Probably End Up Somewhere Else.* Valencia, Calif.: Tabor Publishing, 1974.

Cockrum, Logan V., and Albert C. Winn. *Where Do I Go from Here?* Chicago: Science Research Associates, Inc., 1972.

Farnham, Suzanne G., Joseph P. Gill, R. Taylor McLean, and Susan M. Ward. *Listening Hearts: Discerning Call in Community.* Harrisburg, Pa.: Morehouse Publishing, 1991.

Harris, Marcia B., and Sharon L. Jones. *The Parent's Crash Course in Career Planning.* Lincolnwood, Ill.: NTC Publishing Group, 1994.

Keirsey, David, and Marilyn Bates. *Please Understand Me II: Temperament, Character, and Intelligence.* Del Mar, Calif.: Prometheus Nemesis, 1998.

Levine, Arthur, and Jeanette S. Cureton. *When Hope and Fear Collide: A Portrait of Today's College Student.* San Francisco: Jossey-Bass Publishers, 1997.

Lewis, Roy. *Choosing Your Career, Finding Your Vocation.* Mahwah, N.J.: Paulist Press, 1989.

Lore, Nicholas. *The Pathfinder: How to Choose or Change Your Career for a Lifetime of Satisfaction and Success.* New York: Simon & Schuster, 1998.

O'Brien, Jack. *Next Step: The Real World: Aggressive Tactics to Get Your Professional Life Off to a Fast Start.* Washington, D.C.: Kiplinger, 1999.

Palmer, Parker J. *The Active Life: Wisdom for Work, Creativity, and Caring.* San Francisco: Harper & Row, 1990.

———. *Let Your Life Speak: Listening for the Voice of Vocation.* San Francisco: Jossey-Bass, 2000.

Realizing the Dream: Career Planning for the Twenty-first Century. Iowa City: The American College Testing Program and the National Career Development Association, 1994.

Setzer, Sue M. *What Will I Do with My Life?* Philadelphia: Parish Life Press, 1986.

Tieger, Paul D., and Barbara Barron-Tieger. *Do What You Are: Discover the Perfect Career for You through the Secrets of Personality Type.* Boston: Little, Brown and Co., 1992.

Faith Development and Spirituality

Arsenault, Jane E., and Jean R. Cedor. *Guided Meditations for Youth on the Sacramental Life.* Winona, Minn.: Saint Mary's Press, 1993.

Bass, Dorothy C., ed. *Practicing Our Faith: A Way of Life for a Searching People.* San Francisco: Jossey-Bass, 1997.

Dean, Kenda Creasy, and Ron Foster. *The Godbearing Life: The Art of Soul Tending for Youth Ministry.* Nashville: Upper Room Books, 1998.

Edwards, Tilden. *Sabbath Time.* Nashville: Upper Room Books, 1992.

Everding, H. Edward, Jr., Mary M. Wilcox, Lucinda A. Huffaker, and Clarence H. Snelling, Jr. *Viewpoints: Perspectives of Faith and Christian Nurture.* Harrisburg, Pa.: Trinity Press International, 1998.

Fowler, James W. *Stages of Faith.* San Francisco: Harper & Row, 1981, See especially pp. 98–213.

Gribbon, Robert T. *Developing Faith in Young Adults: Effective Ministry with 18–35 Year Olds.* Washington, D.C.: The Alban Institute, 1990.

Johnson, Ben Campbell. *Listening for God: Spiritual Directives for Searching Christians.* New York: Paulist Press, 1997.

———. *Living before God: Deepening Our Sense of the Divine Presence.* Grand Rapids: Wm. B. Eerdmans Publishing Co., 2000.

Loring, Patricia. *Listening Spirituality.* Vol. I: *Personal Spiritual Practices among Friends.* Washington, D.C.: Openings Press, 1997.

Marcum, Walt. *Living in the Light.* Nashville: Abingdon Press, 1994.

Parks, Sharon. *The Critical Years: The Young Adult Search for a Faith to Live By.* New York: Harper & Row, 1986.

Shelton, Charles M. *Adolescent Spirituality: Pastoral Ministry for High School and College Youth.* New York: Crossroad, 1983.

Thompson, Marjorie J. *Family: The Forming Center.* Nashville: Upper Room Books, 1996.

———. *Soul Feast: An Invitation to the Christian Spiritual Life.* Louisville, Ky.: Westminster John Knox Press, 1995.

Vitek, John M. *A Companion Way: Mentoring Youth in Searching Faith.* Winona, Minn.: Saint Mary's Press, 1992.

Westerhoff, John H. *Will Our Children Have Faith?* New York: Seabury Press, 1976. See especially pp. 89–103.

Wuthnow, Robert. *After Heaven: Spirituality in America since the 1950s.* Los Angeles: University of California Press, 1998.

Generational Studies

Barna, George. *Baby Busters: The Disillusioned Generation.* Chicago: Northfield Publishing, 1994.

———. *Generation Next: What You Need to Know about Today's Youth.* Ventura, Calif.: Regal Books, 1995.

Rainer, Thom S. *The Bridger Generation.* Nashville: Broadman and Holman Publishers, 1997.

Straus, William, and Neil Howe. *The Fourth Turning.* New York: Broadway Books, 1997.

———. *Generations: The History of America's Future, 1584 to 2069.* New York: William Morrow and Co., 1991.

———. *Thirteenth Gen: Abort, Retry, Ignore, Fail?* New York: Vintage Books, 1993.

Disabilities or Special-Needs Persons

Bolles, Richard Nelson. *Job-Hunting Tips for the So-Called Handicapped or Persons Who Have Disabilities.* Berkley, Calif.: Ten Speed Press, 1991.

Fowler, Mary. *CHADD Educator's Manual: An In-Depth Look at Attention Deficit Disorders from an Educational Perspective.* Fairfax, Va.: CASET Associates, 1992.

Goldman, Charles D., Esq. *Disability Rights Guide.* Lincoln, Neb.: Media Publishing, 1991.

Gostin, Lawrence O., and Henry A. Boyce. *Implementing the Americans with Disabilities Act.* Baltimore: Paul Brookes Publishing, 1993.

Kutz-Mellem, Sharon, ed. *Different Members, One Body: Welcoming the Diversity of Abilities in God's Family.* Louisville, Ky.: Witherspoon Press, 1998.

Project Faith, c/o Roswell Presbyterian Church, 755 Mimosa Blvd., Roswell, GA 30075. Telephone: (770) 717-8929 or (770) 663-7274 (voice mail).

Internet Resources

Internet resources abound. New ones emerge regularly. Web sites available today may not be available tomorrow, as Web site addresses and titles change frequently. In this section, we list a few sites that we have found helpful.

For those new to the Internet, here's how to find career-related Web sites:

1. Use a search engine, a tool designed to speed the search process. Some search engines give multiple search results, showing the results of searches done on other search engines. Examples of search engines:

Dogpile	www.dogpile.com
Altavista	www.altavista.com
Yahoo	www.yahoo.com
Lycos	www.lycos.com
Ask Jeeves	www.ask.com
Northern Light	www.northernlight.com
Google	www.google.com

2. Type in a keyword to search, such as "careers," "career counseling," "career guidance," "special needs," or "disabilities." A list of the search results—names of Web sites, organizations, and companies—will appear on your screen. These names, called hyperlinks, will be highlighted in color and underlined. Click on a particular hyperlink and it will take you to the Web site.

3. When you reach a Web site, you may notice other references (hyperlinks) listed, which will take you to other Web sites.

Sites for Career Counseling Helps

What Color is Your Parachute? Job Hunting Online
  www.tenspeed.com or www.jobhuntersbible.com

Keirsey Temperament Sorter
  www.keirsey.com

Myers-Briggs
  www.paladinexec.com

Career Resource Homepage
  www.rpi.edu/dept/cdc/homepage.html

The Occupational Outlook Handbook
  http://stats.bls.gov/ocohome.htm

Monster Campus
  http://campus.monster.com

My Future
  www.myfuture.com

Sites for Job Listings

JobBank USA MetaSEARCH
  www.jobbankusa.com/search.html

America's Job Bank
  www.ajb.dni.us

Career Path
  www.careerpath.com

CareerSite.com
  www.careersite.com

The Monster Board Career Search
  www.monster.com

Nonprofit Resources Catalog
  www.nonprofits.org

Site for Volunteering and Internships

4Work
  www.4work.com

Internet Sites for Special Needs

The Mining Company
  http://specialchildren.miningco.com

Careers On-Line
  http://disserv3.stu.umn.edu/COL

Work Inc
  www.workinc.org

Independent Homeworkers Alliance
  www.homeworkers.org

Interdenominational Career Development Centers

The Career and Personal Counseling Center
4108 Park Road, Suite 200
Charlotte, NC 28209
704-523-7751

The Career and Personal Counseling Center
Eckerd College
St. Petersburg, FL 33733
813-864-8356

Career Development Center of the Southeast
531 Kirk Road
Decatur, GA 30030
404-371-0336

Center for Career Development and Ministry
70 Chase Street
Newton Center, MA 02159
617-969-7750

The Center for Ministry
8393 Capwell Drive, Suite 220
Oakland, CA 94621-2123
510-635-4246

Mid-Atlantic Career Center, Inc.
1401 Columbia
Lancaster, PA 17603
717-397-7451

Midwest Career Development Service
1840 Westchester Blvd., Suite 204
Westchester, IL 60154-1334
708-343-6268

Midwest Career Development Service
1520 Old Henderson Road, Suite 102B
Columbus, OH 43220-3639
614-442-8822

Midwest Ministry Development Service
754 North 31st Street
Kansas City, KS 66110-0816
913-621-6348

North Central Career Development Center
516 Mission House Lane
New Brighton, MN 55112
612-636-5120

Northeast Career Center
407 Nassau Street
Princeton, NJ 08540
609-924-9408

Southwest Career Development Center
624 Six Flags Drive, Suite 210
Arlington, TX 76011
817-649-8134

NOTES

Chapter 1: The Church's Unique Opportunity

1. Kenda Creasy Dean and Ron Foster, *The Godbearing Life: The Art of Soul Tending for Youth Ministry* (Nashville: Upper Room Books, 1998), 46.
2. Barna Research Group identifies Generation X, the baby-buster generation, as those born between 1965 and 1983 and Millennials as those born after 1983. William Straus and Neil Howe's research (*Generations: The History of America's Future, 1584 to 2069* [New York: William Morrow and Co., 1991]) uses 1961 to 1981 for Generation X and 1982 to 2003 for Millennials.
3. George Barna, *Baby Busters: The Disillusioned Generation* (Chicago: Northfield Publishing, 1994), 35–36.
4. Thom S. Rainer, *The Bridger Generation* (Nashville: Broadman and Holman Publishers, 1997).
5. Ibid., 9.
6. George Barna, *Generation Next: What You Need to Know about Today's Youth* (Ventura, Calif.: Regal Books, 1995), 64. The 1995 Barna research shows results of a nationwide telephone survey of a random sampling of teenagers, ages thirteen to eighteen, from lower-, middle-, and upper-class households, churched and unchurched, Christian and non-Christian, teens who were Caucasian, African American, Asian American, and Hispanic American.
7. Barbara Kantrowitz and Pat Wingert, "How Well Do You Know Your Kid," *Newsweek*, May 1999, 38–39.
8. Barna, *Generation Next*, 20.
9. Kantrowitz and Wingert, "How Well Do You Know Your Kid," 39.
10. Arthur Levine and Jeanette S. Cureton, *When Hope and Fear Collide: A Portrait of Today's College Student* (San Francisco: Jossey-Bass Publishers, 1997), 38.
11. Barna, *Generation Next*, 27.
12. Martin E. Marty, "'Who Is Jesus Christ for Us Today?' as Asked by Young People," from *The 1998 Princeton Lectures on Youth, Church, and Culture*, 36.
13. Rodger Nishioka, "Surprise! We're Listening and We Care!" *Presbyterian Young Adult Ministry Newsletter*, vol. 1, no. 2 (April 1998).
14. Barna, *Baby Busters*, 45.
15. Ibid., 49.
16. Handt Hanson, "Worship for the Next Generation," *Presbyterian Young Adult Ministry Newsletter*, vol. 1, no. 1 (February 1998).
17. Dean and Foster, *Godbearing Life*, 62.
18. Henri J. M. Nouwen in *The Lord is Near: Advent Meditations from the Works of Henri J. M. Nouwen*, ed. Mark Neilsen (St. Louis: Creative Communications for the Parish, 1993), 7.

Chapter 2: God's Call

1. Ben Campbell Johnson, *Listening for God: Spiritual Directives for Searching Christians* (New York: Paulist Press, 1997), 63.
2. Frederick Buechner, *Wishful Thinking: A Theological ABC* (New York: Harper & Row, 1973), 95.
3. Sister Elizabeth Liebert. "Becoming a Discerning Person" (address at Oasis 2000, Atlanta, February 29, 2000).
4. See "Guidelines for Discernment Groups," in Suzanne G. Farnham, Joseph P. Gill, R. Taylor McLean, and Susan M. Ward, *Listening Hearts: Discerning Call in Community* (Harrisburg, Pa.: Morehouse Publishing, 1991), 77–94. In the Quaker tradition, such groups are called "clearness committees."

Chapter 3: The Practices of Faith

1. Kenda Creasy Dean and Ron Foster, *The Godbearing Life: The Art of Soul Tending for Youth Ministry* (Nashville: Upper Room Books, 1998), 107.
2. Ibid., 106.
3. See Robert Wuthnow, *After Heaven: Spirituality in America since the 1950s* (Los Angeles: University of California Press, 1998).
4. Patricia Loring, *Listening Spirituality,* vol 1: *Personal Spiritual Practices among Friends* (Washington, D.C.: Openings Press, 1997), 170.
5. Kathleen Norris, *Dakota* (1993), quoted in Paula J. Carlson and Peter S. Hawkins, ed., *Listening for God*, vol. 2 (Minneapolis: Augsburg Fortress, 1996), 126.
6. Dean and Foster, *Godbearing Life*, 119.
7. Ibid., 119–120.
8. Loring, *Listening Spirituality*, 130.
9. Ibid., 112.
10. Ibid.
11. Ibid., 131.

Chapter 4: A Design for Career Counseling Ministry with Youth and Young Adults

1. The Keirsey Temperament Sorter II can be found in *Please Understand Me II: Temperament, Character,*

Intelligence, by David Keirsey (Del Mar, Calif.: Prometheus Nemesis, 1998), 4–12.

Chapter 5: Involving Parents, Stepparents, and Guardians

1. Marjorie J. Thompson, *Family: The Forming Center* (Nashville: Upper Room Books, 1996), 59.
2. Susan Mitchell, "The Next Baby Boom," *American Demographics,* vol. 17, no. 10 (October 1995): 27. Cited in Thom S. Rainer, *The Bridger Generation* (Nashville: Broadman and Holman Publishers, 1997), 12.
3. Interview with Ellen Galinsky, author of *Ask the Children: What America's Children Really Think about Working Parents* (New York: William Morrow and Company, 1999), on NBC's *Today* show, 17 September 1999.
4. Nella Barkley, *How to Help Your Child Land the Right Job (without Being a Pain in the Neck)* (New York: Workman Publishing, 1993), 38.

Chapter 7: Adapting Career Counseling Ministry to Youth and Young Adults with Special Needs

1. Peter Marshall and Tina, interview by Forrest Palmer, Lilburn, Ga., 29 September 1998.
2. See "A Brief History of American Disability Act (ADA)" Office of Disability Services Web site, State University of New York (SUNY) at Buffalo, 1999; www.ub-disability.buffalo.edu/moreods.html.

Chapter 11: Session 4—About You: Values, Lifestyles, and Risk

1. Sean Covey, *The Seven Habits of Highly Effective Teens* (New York: Simon & Schuster, 1998), 117.

Chapter 12: Session 5—The World of Work: Career Fields

1. See John L. Holland, *Making Vocational Choices: Third Edition: A Theory of Vocational Personalities and Work Environments* (Odessa, Fla.: Psychological Assessment Resources, Inc., 1997).

Chapter 14: Staying on the Journey

1. Missy Bernall, *She Said Yes* (Farmington, Pa.: The Plough Publishing House, 1999), ix.

Appendix 1: The Journal

1. Stacy Johnson, "The Image of God and Our Spiritual Journey" (address at Oasis 2000, Atlanta, March 1, 2000).
2. Parker J. Palmer, *Let Your Life Speak: Listening for the Voice of Vocation* (San Francisco: Jossey-Bass, 2000), 3.
3. Walter Brueggemann. "Miracle and Accommodation: The Story of a Military Man" (address at Oasis 2000, Atlanta, February 29, 2000).
4. Sister Elizabeth Liebert. "Becoming a Discerning Person" (address at Oasis 2000, Atlanta, February 29, 2000).
5. Andrew Dreitcer. "Resources of Grace for the Spiritual Journey" (address at Oasis 2000, Atlanta, March 1, 2000).
6. Palmer, *Let Your Life Speak,* 30.
7. Frederick Buechner, *Wishful Thinking: A Theological ABC* (New York: Harper & Row, 1973) 95.
8. Palmer, *Let Your Life Speak,* 10.
9. Henri J. M. Nouwen, *The Lord is Near: Advent Meditations from the Works of Henri J. M. Nouwen,* ed. Mark Neilsen (St. Louis: Creative Communications for the Parish, 1993), 3.
10. Palmer, *Let Your Life Speak,* 54.
11. Ben Campbell Johnson. "Imagining a Church in the Spirit" (address at First Presbyterian Church's Officers Retreat, Atlanta, February 12, 2000).

Appendix 2: A Spirituality Retreat

1. Bernie Siegel, M.D., *Guided Imagery and Meditation* (New Haven, Conn.: ECAP, 1986).
2. Walt Marcum, *Living in the Light* (Nashville: Abingdon Press, 1994).